Sexual Dimensions of the Celibate Life

WILLIAM KRAFT

Sexual Dimensions
of the Celibate Life

ANDREWS AND McMEEL, INC.
A Universal Press Syndicate Company
KANSAS CITY

Library of Congress Cataloging in Publication Data
Kraft, William F   1938-
  Sexual dimensions of the celibate life.

  Bibliography: p.
  1. Celibacy.   2. Love.   3. Marriage.
4. Single people—Sexual behavior.   5. Intimacy
(Psychology)   6. Loneliness.   I. Title.
HQ800.K72   301.41'7   79-270
ISBN 0-8362-3908-3

FOR
Billy and Jennifer

Contents

Preface

Celibacy is neither popular nor encouraged. Many persons scoff at the idea of celibate sexuality, or consider it an impossibility, a sign of immaturity, or simply sad. Some celibates reluctantly accept, miserably endure, or resentfully hate their life. And both celibates and noncelibates often assume that celibacy and marriage are mutually exclusive. Yet, there are those who freely accept and vow celibacy, proclaim its value, and live happy and significant lives, as well as those who value celibacy as a necessary and significant part of marriage.

Academically, clinically, and personally, I have journeyed in many worlds of celibacy. Religious have helped me to appreciate the problems, joys, and significance of being a vowed celibate. Single men and women have shared their celibate pain and pleasure, and married persons have shown me the meaning of celibacy in marriage. Although celibacy was found to be infinitely more than a sexual issue, sexuality, along with loneliness and intimacy, often emerged as a crucial obstacle to and opportunity for growth. Many questions and problems emerged, but relatively few answers and solutions, particularly concrete and constructive ones, were evident. So, I explored the worlds of celibate sexuality—and, I believe, discovered helpful ways to cope with and enjoy celibate sexuality.

Initially, this book was to be written for religious because they vow celibacy. But then many single and married persons urged me to speak to them as well. The result is a book on celibate sexuality in the married, religious, and single lives.

These are other reasons why I, whose primary commitment is to my wife and two children, wrote this book. I was a lay celibate before I married, and I contend that marriage does and should incorporate celibacy. Thus, this book is also a personal project, and it can be helpful to married people as well as to celibates.

The book presents a basic theory of sexuality and an implicit vision of personhood, and then three modes of sexuality are explored—primary, affective, and genital. In light of this framework, celibate situations, which often apply to married people, are analyzed along with areas such as love and sexuality, normal and abnormal sexual madness, and sexual emergence throughout the life cycle.

My thanks are offered to many men and women. Colleauges, students, clients, and friends motivated me to make concrete and relevant sense. Teachers, particularly Bernard Boelen, Bert van Croonenberg, and Adrian van Kaam, offered me valuable insights into the mystery of being human. I am also grateful to Patricia Kraft and Suzanne McClintock for their views and research, to Elizabeth Bartelme for her editing, and to Denise Kroll and Margie McGuirk for their typing. I humbly thank Mom, Dad, Jennifer, Billy, and Pat for accepting and loving a "married celibate."

CHAPTER I

Celibacy and Sexuality

Listen to this twenty-nine-year-old woman. "My divorce was the most difficult thing I've ever done. The trauma for me and my kids, and I think for my husband too, was excruciating. And though I never believed in divorce, I felt that a marriage where people were killing each other was worse than any divorce. Sure, it's easy to say now that I got married when I was too young. Although I was almost a legal adult, twenty, I was far from being a mature person. But we did it—and we had children.

"It's been two years since my divorce, and things are settling down a bit. I've somehow learned to manage to get by on half the income that I previously had, and I think I'm a little more fortunate than many women in that I got a half-decent job. Still, I might add that I'm not paid nearly the same as a man who is doing a comparable job. But we are managing. And I'm lucky that the kids are in good schools. So, I feel the future promises better things for us.

"Let me be candid. Sometimes I crave sex. Sometimes my desires seem almost purely physical—anybody will do. I want more than anything to make love, to touch, climax, sleep with somebody. I feel that I should be embarrassed to say this, but I'm really not. I've had two relationships in the past year. No, I'm not going to the local bar to be picked up, though I can understand women who do this. I've met a couple of nice guys who honestly propose—and I agree—that we have a short-term relationship and enjoy and appreciate each other. We have fun, and it really is good to be cared for and to care. Certainly, the relationship is not all sexual, but sex is an important part of it. When we part, there is some disappointment and pain, but this is what we agreed to, so it seems to ease the pain. Yet, am I destined to go throughout life having affairs? I hate to call them that; it sounds so cheap. They're more than that. But when the relationship is over, I have to admit that I do feel empty. It seems that nothing lasts.

"I have no qualms about getting married again. But this time, I'm going to be sure—at least I'll try to be—to know what I'm getting into. But look, I'm twenty-nine. I'm still fairly young, but losing my youth quickly. Soon, very soon, I will be thirty, and try to get married when you have two kids and you're thirty. Sure, I suppose you can get married if you're willing to get married to almost anyone. But I've already traveled that dead-end route.

"I really don't know what's going to happen, and it scares me. I want to get married, but I want to have a good and happy marriage. And I feel the odds are against this. So, what do I do? Do I try to raise my kids, and periodically have some sort of relationship? Do I try to be a single mother? Do I masturbate when sexuality becomes intense? Believe me, masturbation is a poor substitute for another person. Can you tell me where I can find an available mature man? Can you tell me what I should do with my yearnings for intimacy and, yes, sexual intimacy too? Should I accept my lot and live through it? Somehow life is too short for that. What should I do? Can you tell me?"

This woman does not want to be celibate, and she finds herself in a quandary. Sexual relationships do give some meaning and satisfaction, but the meaning and fulfillment do not last. She feels the pain of permanency in its absence. She also feels that she is growing older, and the pressures, often sexist, are against her. She chooses to be divorced in lieu of a marital charade, yet she does not want to be celibate. What chance does she really have? If she does not get married, what can she do with her longings for intimacy?

"To say the least, my parents were not exactly enthusiastic when I told them I planned to become a nun. They said they knew I was thinking about entering religious life, but they never thought I would go through with it. Of course, they said they wanted what was best for me and what would make me happy, but I have to give them credit, they did speak their minds.

They asked me if I really knew what I was doing. Was I really willing to give up married life, a husband and children? Would I be happy living a life of poverty, obedience, and celibate chastity? My father wondered out loud, and asked me if the celibate life was the one for me. My first impulse was to confront them with the realities of married life. I wanted to ask them how many marriages are really happy and fulfilling. I wanted to say that married life is often no big deal. But really, this was not my reason for entering religious life. I simply felt I was called and that I would like the life. I felt that the religious life was the best way for me to be happy and to live a complete life.

"I soon found that my decision to enter religious life was far from popular. My older brother shook his head in apparent disgust, and my younger sister thought I was stupid. Some of my relatives gave me lukewarm approval, and others just seemed indifferent. My friends also pointed out the fun and opportunities I would be missing. At first, the guy I was dating was really shocked. Although he kind of knew it was coming, he was hurt. And my decision hurt me, too; I still hurt when I think about us. But I felt if I didn't at least give the religious life a try, I'd be doing myself and him an injustice. I really couldn't say much, only that I loved him but couldn't marry him.

"All that seems like a thousand years ago, though it was only about fifteen years ago. Now I am thirty-six. Religious life has been good to me, and I hope I have been good to it. I have precious friends, and I think I've done some good work. More importantly, I feel I have grown closer to God and to people. But my father's haunting question comes back to me: Can I really live a celibate life? The experts say that I am at the peak of my sexual life, and I believe them. I'm really at a loss as to what to do with my sexual feelings. Sometimes when I am lonely, I yearn to be held by a man and to hold him. I have to admit that I wonder what it would be like to have loving sex with a man. I know that this is contrary to my commitment. Yet, I still have my yearnings to be intimate, my desires to give and to be given to.

"Yes, I know one of the latest theories is to integrate sexuality. But nobody says how. Integration is a nice word, but how in God's name do you do it. I tried masturbation, but that really didn't do any good. It did relieve some tension, but it only seemed to make things worse. And furthermore, I still feel uncomfortable with masturbation. I don't have guilt feelings like I did when I was an adolescent, but somehow I feel masturbation is not the best way to cope with my sexuality.

"Here I am, trying to lead a good religious life, and many people say that I do. I am a celibate for the kingdom of God, but I am also sexual, very much so. Sometimes I get the feeling that I am the only one like me. Yet I know that most sisters, it not all, have somewhat the same problems as I. Still, we seldom if ever talk about it. Sure, sometimes we'll imply some things or a few friends will talk about it, but seldom are the cards put on the table and something concrete done about it. I feel so alone with my sexuality."

Unlike the single parent, this religious sister vowed celibacy. She believes that a vowed and celibate life in a religious community is the best way she can live. She is a vibrant woman who is living a meaningful religious life and doing good for others, but her sexual search is frustrating. She gets little help from her community and she wonders where she can find it. She often feels that everybody is trying to pretend that sexual problems do not exist within religious life. Or, with good intentions on the part of the adviser, she may be told to pray and have faith. Although she appreciates the concern of others and believes in prayer, she feels that more should be done. This sister is given help in her spiritual life, but the incarnational, sexual aspect of her personality receives relatively little recognition.

Listen to this man. "Celibacy—why in the world would somebody choose that? What do I think people like nuns, brothers, and priests do with their sexuality? My guess is that some masturbate or mess around, or otherwise they repress and become irritable and frustrated. Really, I don't know what they do. I don't know how they could be happy or healthy without sex. Isn't that abnormal?

"I guess you could call me a celibate in the sense that I'm not married. But I do have an active sex life. And really, sex is not that difficult to find. Just a little effort, not much, and you can get it. Look, there are a lot of places where chicks are just waiting to be shown a good time and are willing to give a little in return. If you want sex and you're not getting it, it's your own fault. A celibate life? It's one of the more ridiculous and wasteful things I've heard of.

"Yes, I've been married twice. No more of that for me. Much too much hassle, and for what? If I didn't have these damn payments, I'd really be in good shape. But soon that will be over with, and I'll really be on easy street. Look, I have my own place, sports car, I practically go wherever I want to. What's better than that?

"Have you ever gone on a Vegas junket? Now, that's life. Chicks who are really with it and know what to do. A good life. And when it's over, no strings attached. No downs, always ups. No hassles, no bitching, no kids, none of that crap. Sure, I guess I'm going to the extreme. I guess a few people are happily married, but I don't see very many. My point is that you can be a single person and have a good sex life.

"Okay. I know I'm getting older. I'm forty-nine; I really can't say I'm young. But I'm still not old. I guess I have to admit that I'm not what I used to be. And, since you're listening, I admit that I have to pay a little more than I used to. But what the hell, that's the way it goes. If you have the money, you can get anything you want. Me, lonely? I guess I am sometimes, but who isn't? And of course, there's always masturbation. Sure, it's not as good as a chick, but it does help. What do I do with my sexuality? What else? I satisfy it."

This man's life and approach to sex differ radically from the sister and the divorced woman. In some ways, he could be called a single, noncelibate person who has an active sexual life, and yet he is celibate in that he is unmarried and lives alone. When he desires sex, he finds a woman or he masturbates. He claims to have no problems with sex.

Think of this thirty-nine-year-old man. "When my wife died, I almost died. It's really good to be able to say that we were happy with each other. I am thankful, but I still feel somewhat lost and very lonely. I am indeed fortunate to have lived with and to have loved such a wonderful woman for fifteen years, and to have three fine children. And though I know my wife is still with me, I can't really touch and feel, laugh and play with, talk with and listen to her. This hurts and hurts and hurts.

"I don't think I really want to get married again, but I find myself reaching out for someone. Should I get married again? I'm no longer young; in fact, I am close to middle age. Still, I know how easy it is to enter a relationship with a woman, short or long term. In some ways, I think this would ease my pain. And yet, somehow I feel that if I could make love to a woman, almost any woman, things would be better. Sometimes the yearning is great, and I really don't know what to do. Alcohol seems to help, but it only numbs the pain and solves nothing. I never thought I would live a celibate life. When I take stock of myself, I wonder if I am strong enough to be a good celibate, or if I need or want to be one.

"What do I do with my longings for intimacy? How do I answer my questions of loneliness? Can I be happy and alone? What do I do when a woman invites me to be intimate with her? I'm not saying this in a cheap way, because the several times this has happened the women have been good people. And it is awfully tempting. Would it be so wrong to enter a few relationships? Whom would I be hurting? Some of my colleagues think I'm crazy for not accepting such invitations. But something says no to me. If I do say no to sexual intimacy, what do I do with my sexual feelings? Do I just numb them? I don't like numbing myself. What is the answer?"

This man did not choose celibacy; it was thrust upon him. He never thought he would be leading a celibate life, nor does he want to. Unlike the religious sister, he did not freely choose to live a celibate life, nor does he live in a community that supports and nourishes him. And he may have more opportunities and pressures to enter sexual relationships. Unlike the divorced man, he did not choose to be single and does not engage in sexual affairs. In a situation more similar to that of the religious and lay woman than to the single man, this widower also wonders what he should do with his sexuality.

"Well, what do you do with sex if you want to remain celibate? Here I am, twenty-one years old, almost a college graduate, and still a virgin. It's stupid, but I feel almost embarrassed or as if I have to appologize because I've had no sexual relations. I know that virginity is not the most popular thing on campus and that I may be considered old-fashioned. But for whatever reason, I still think premarital sex is wrong for me. It may sound stupid, but I want to wait until marriage. Sure, I have to admit I'd like to try it. Sometimes I really get horny, and it's awfully tempting. Why do I sometimes feel one way and think another?

"Sure, guys and girls give me the argument that it all depends on the situation. You know, if two people are honest and sincere about their relationship and don't hurt anyone, then what's wrong with having sex? As long as you don't exploit another, sex is okay. Besides, they say it is a natural drive that should be satisfied. What am I? Unnatural? I can't give them much of an argument. I can only say that since I wouldn't recommend premarital sex to my future kids, I wouldn't practice it myself."

Is this young adult necessarily puritanical, stupid, or out of touch with modern times? Is it necessary for her to feel embarrassed about her celibacy? If not, what can she do with her sexuality? What can she say to herself and others in support of her celibate stand?

We can begin to see that there are many modes of celibate living and that people are celibate for various reasons. Some people choose to be celibate for life and others choose celibacy for a temporary period of time. Some do not choose celibacy, but reluctantly abstain from genital behavior, while others engage in genital relationships. To make sense of celibate sexuality, first consider the meaning of celibacy.

CELIBACY

Celibates are persons who may live either alone or in a community, but who do not have a permanent commitment to live with another human being. Consequently, a celibate does not have the daily and exclusive concern and support from another individual that a married person can expect. Nor do celibates have the opportunity for intimacy within a home situation. Normally they do not have access to genital sexuality such as is available to married persons. Indeed, married people can be semi- or complete celibates in that they may have little or no genital sexuality in their marriage and may live very separate lives. Furthermore, we will see that marriage includes celibate experiences that are similar to and different from the single and religious life experiences. Basically, however, celibate persons lack the exclusive and relatively constant concern and support of a marriage partner.

Celibacy, however, does not simply denote an unmarried status. In a more positive sense, celibacy (which etymologically means to be alone) can also be a distinct and meaningful life form. As single individuals, celibates are more likely than married people to be alone. Although they may live in a community and have friends, celibates, more than normal married persons, usually experience more solitude and loneliness which, however, can foster self-discovery and life appreciation. The celibate life-style and situation usually affords more opportunity to listen in aloneness and loneliness than does the married life. This does not mean to imply that celibates are recluses, but that their daily experiences usually differ somewhat from those of married persons.

The celibate mode of living should increase the likelihood of experiencing transcendent values that support and promote love. For instance, the celibate life usually encourages silence, and silence encourages listening. Celibates should have more opportunities for recollection, meditation, contemplation, and other experiences that promote love. Indeed, celibacy usually involves more lonely aloneness. Nevertheless, celibates can be guardians and vanguards of love.

A celibate life can also liberate persons to be more accessible to others as contrasted to being accessible mainly to one other. Being free from a commitment to one other can increase freedom for others. Celibates have more time and energy than married persons to invest in activities outside their community. For instance, they may often be freer for leisure and service involvements beyond their personal and work situations.

Furthermore, celibates are usually freer to pursue their own interests than is the average married person. Besides leisure and social involvements, celibates usually have more time and energy to invest in aesthetic, spiritual, literary, scholarly, avocational, and other such activities. Married persons, especially if they have children, usually do not have as much opportunity for reading or scholarly research as do many celibates, although in some cases where one of the spouses (most often the woman) takes most of the domestic responsibility, the other spouse may be able to dedicate (himself) to a career. Usually, however, to be a good spouse and parent, a person must invest time and energy in the marriage that is then not available for other activities.

In terms of the boundaries we have set, there is a sizeable number of celibates in our society. In fact, there seems to be a growing trend toward the celibate life. Some people may argue that divorced persons or swinging singles are not celibate. Within our framework, however, these people are celibate: they are unmarried and essentially alone. We have already indicated that the reasons for being unmarried or celibate can vary considerably. The motivations and circumstances of each life differentiate the kind' of celibacy, and the motivations for each celibate life-style vary considerably. Let us consider some of the various kinds of celibacy.

Modes of Celibate Living

We have indicated that there are various reasons for being celibate. For instance, widowed persons are involuntary celibates, who, though they chose to be married, find themselves living as celibates. Divorced individuals may also want to be married, but they choose celibacy because they think it is better than an unhappy married life. Separation can be a poor person's way of being divorced, a transitional step to a divorce, or a moratorium that will eventually be in service of a reunion. Whatever the case, separated people are also celibate.

There are other reasons for being single, such as being too young to be married. Obviously, children and most teenagers neither have the opportunity nor the maturity to marry. Such celibacy is neither voluntary nor involuntary because in their situation the choice does not arise. Others who are single may be so because of parental pressures or responsibilities to parents. Still others may unconsciously withdraw from the possibility of a marital commitment because of fear or poor self-esteem. Although they choose to be celibate, their decision is not free.

Some adults choose to be celibate because they do not feel called to the married life. Others feel that married life is a farce, for having observed many transitory and phony marriages they come to feel that happy marriages and permanent commitments are illusions. Other voluntary lay celibates may choose a single life because of its freedom, and because they believe that the single life can include sexuality. Although they may have active sex lives, they are unmarried and in this sense celibate.

Some people are ready and willing to marry but are unlikely to do so. For example, an unfair and often sexist situation exists for many adult women. In order to discover oneself and thereby have a greater possibility of a healthy and happy marriage, a person usually needs time. But if a woman waits until her late twenties and especially until her thirties to marry, the opportunities of meeting a mature and free man are very limited. There are many solid, mature, and dignified women who want to get married but cannot meet a man of equal worth for a permanent relationship. If such women were willing to take less than what is best, they would not have as much difficulty. But their dignity demands that they find a worthy spouse or remain celibate. These women do not like their celibacy, but they would rather be celibate than unhappily married.

Religious are another group of celibates. These people freely commit themselves to a (celibate) life that includes the vows of poverty, obedience, and chastity within the context of community living. Although these celibates are a minority in terms of numbers, their life has a unique quality. Besides witnessing to a vow and to a community, they also give witness to the value of celibate living. They explicitly proclaim to society that celibate living can have significant value. Religious commit themselves to a vowed, communal, celibate life because they believe their celibacy frees them for a life of love for others and for God. Some special attention is given to these religious because they publicly choose and proclaim the value of celibate living.

Religious are celibates primarily for the kingdom of God. They feel that their celibacy in community helps them to grow spiritually—to love God and others more than a nonreligious life would normally afford them. Married and single persons can also declare that their life is for the kingdom of God, but they neither publicly vow celibacy nor live in a religious community. Still, religious are not altogether different from other celibates. Although their motivation for being celibate differs, they stand on the same ground as other celibates and have the same feelings, including sexual feelings.

Many priests, particularly Roman Catholics, also choose and proclaim the value of a celibate life. Unlike religious, however, they do not usually take a vow of poverty nor are they members of a religious community. Although their life-style usually differs from that of most religious, such priests are committed celibates. Similarly, some lay single persons also freely choose the celibate life, but they usually do not take public vows or live in a community.

CELIBACY AND MARRIAGE

Listen to this married woman. "I really think that celibacy is the purest form of life. By that I mean a celibate has fewer distractions and demands than a married person. Having no husband and children and all that, this means you can have more freedom to do other things. Not only that, but by 'pure' I also mean you are thrown back on yourself. It's really up to you to live a meaningful life."

Celibate man: "Yes, I see what you mean, and there's truth in what you say. But, it's easy for you—a married person—to say that. You have a husband and children to support you. Think of going home to an empty house. There's no one there to say hello, no one to share the day's problems with. If you have a rough day, you can at least talk to someone. There's always someone there to listen and help. I realize that most married people have a lot of problems. And sometimes I wonder if a happy marriage is really possible. Still, I'm alone."

Married woman: "True, somewhat. I still say you have more opportunities. You can get involved in more situations, and you have more time to reflect. I know being alone can be painful, but it has its benefits, too. And you realize that married people are not always together. How do you think it feels to be alone and lonely when you're with someone? And there are times when I want just some rest, some solitude, and it's almost impossible. I'm just saying that I also feel alone for various reasons, but I don't have the freedom that you have."

Celibate man: "Don't forget sex. That's something I don't have, and it can solve a lot of problems."

Married woman: "What do you mean? Sex doesn't solve anything. If my husband and I are having problems, sex is the last thing I want. Sure, I guess if sex is only physical, then I might engage. But sex is also emotional. I mean I can't separate sex and love. Having sex when there are problems would cause more problems."

Celibate man: "I'm not talking about purely physical sex. In fact, I think almost any kind of sex, practically anywhere or with anyone, involves more than just the physical. I think there's always some feeling or care. That's why I think a wife should always be available to her husband. One reason is that love means accepting what you don't like or what hurts you. And having sex, even when you don't want to, can heal a lot of hurt."

Married woman: "Just a minute, now. First of all, I don't like your chauvinistic attitude—that a wife should always be available to her husband. That's really old-fashioned. Where is the two-way street? Besides, I don't think you're right. As I said, it doesn't work that way. And what's wrong with hurting? Sometimes it's necessary to suffer pain when it's necessary to improve the marriage. For me, sex would be a way of running from problems, and therefore not help-ing either of us."

Celibate man: "Still, I think the care, as little as it might be, would help. You have to admit that marriage is easier. You do have sex, and that beats loneliness. Sure, I admit that mere physical sex is like masturbation. But it doesn't have to be that way. I don't think anyone wants to be single."

Married woman: "Marriage might be easier, but that doesn't make it better. Still, once again, there's a lot of aloneness in marriage. Sex on demand is a sexist fiction and it's impossible. Sex is only a part of marriage, and it really can't go well unless the other parts are good too."

Celibate Man: "I agree that sex is only a part of life, but it can make a big difference. Do you want to switch places?"

Married woman: "No, thank you."

This married woman has chosen and essentially is happy with her married life, but she also feels that celibacy can be a meaningful alternative. She disagrees with some of the celibate's views on sex, which she judges to be sincere al-though somewhat sexist, naive, and magical. Though she enjoys sex, she thinks that he overestimates its importance and thinks of sex as a panacea. She also hints that marriage includes a kind of celibacy, and she affirms the value of celibacy.

The celibate, who is a good man, tends to consider celi-bacy and marriage as mutually exclusive, as having little in common. And he seems to value marriage over celibacy, even though he admits that few marriages work out or are happy. He seems caught between his frustration as a celi-bate and his scepticism of marriage. Furthermore, this man sees sex as a healing power that helps solve problems and alleviates loneliness.

Listen to this thirty-three year old woman.

"I don't know what has happened to our marriage. It seems like a thousand years ago that we met, but it was only eleven when we seemed to be so much in love. We felt that everything was possible and nothing could stop us. Now, nothing seems possible. Where has our love gone?

"When we got married, we never wanted to separate. We couldn't stand being without each other. Now, we are like strangers who somehow live at the same place. We can't or don't get close to each other. Ha, I thought I felt lonely before I got married; nothing beats this—being lonely and even alone when you're living with someone. While the kids were still at home and I was having babies, I guess I didn't notice what was happening. Now that the kids are in school, I really feel it.

"I feel like I'm always taken for granted. I'm expected to do this, that, whatever, and no one seems to notice. Do they think that everything gets done by accident? And they don't realize how boring and demeaning much of my life can be. What would happen if I didn't cook? What would happen if I didn't slave for a day and a half to cook a Thanksgiving meal that I have to sneak in between football games?

"More important is that I—I—am taken for granted, expected to give, be always there with little respect and appreciation. Sex is a classic. Funny, though I feel more sexual than ever before, we have much less sex than before. It seems that we have sex when it fits into my husband's schedule, which isn't very often. And sex with him is seldom very good. I usually end up more tense and frustrated. How do you think it feels to be more lonely after having sex? Sometimes I wonder if I'm worth anything to anyone. It's tempting to try to find out."

This woman initially felt that marriage was the way to fulfillment, but now she feels empty, harried, lonely, and alone. She feels more like an object than a person. And love is present in its absence. In a sense, she experiences herself as an exploited celibate—somebody that is used to satisfy the needs of others. She wants appreciation, concern, love. And she wonders if she could find it elsewhere.

"I hate to admit it, but I'm terribly scared of being impotent. That's one problem I never thought I'd have. I simply can't perform the way I used to. And worse yet, I seldom have the desire to have sex. And look, I'm not old yet: I'm forty-four. Am I? I always feel so tired. Or there's always something else to do.

"I get the feeling my wife expects more of me and is disappointed with me. God, how I hate to go on vacations. I don't know what to do with her. What if we just went with each other instead of with our kids and our friends' families? I wonder what my wife feels about it. I guess we should talk.

"Why kid myself? We haven't really talked for years. Anyhow, I wouldn't know what to say. I'd feel so embarrassed and weak. Yet, something should be done. Marriage has to be more than a tense adjustment—a keeping out of each other's way. Hell, I was happier when I was single. I was by myself, and sure, I felt lonely, but I wasn't so miserable and alone."

This man wants but is afraid of intimacy. He wants to communicate, but he does not know how and he feels vulnerable. He feels ashamed of his sexual inadequacy and feels helpless and anxious. He dreads what he wants most—love. He dislikes and feels guilty about his "celibacy"—being alone. He feels uncomfortable with being a married single who merely adjusts to living with someone. In fact, he wonders if being a celibate single would be better than his marital charades.

"I'm really happy to say that after twenty years of marriage life is better than ever. My wife and I are more in love and we enjoy living together. Sure, we've had a few ups and downs, but they seemed to work out for the better. We like being alone with each other. And sex is great. We don't have sex quite as often as when we were first married, but sex is much better. It's funny, when I say that I am happily married, people look at me as if I'm giving them a line. Or people ask me why I'm so happy.

"No, we're not always together. That's symbiosis. When I have to go on a trip, I miss my wife. I'm lonely. Some men encourage me to pick up a hooker or at least to masturbate. Sure, this could relieve the immediate discomfort, but it would also lessen my yearning and appreciation for my wife. I don't want to do that. And at home, we accept and give each other the right to be alone. I feel that our aloneness is a way to affirm and nourish ourselves and is essential to growing in love for each other. As Anne Morrow Lindbergh might say, we must take creative pauses away from each other to return creatively for each other."

This man speaks of a different kind of celibacy in marriage. He clearly states that it is necessary to be alone in order to grow in love. He affirms and advocates a form of celibacy in service of actualizing self and other. He feels that ameliorating the pain of loneliness and aloneness would militate against his growing in love with his wife. His loneliness and aloneness (celibacy) actually help him to love more and better.

We can see that although marriage and celibacy are distinct life forms, they are not totally different. Marriage does incorporate, for various reasons, celibacy—times of aloneness. "Marital celibacy" can be a sign of something radically wrong, or it can be good and necessary for personal and interpersonal growth. And celibacy can incorporate community—a love for others and a communion with life. Consider the relation between marriage and celibacy and some of their similarities and differences.

We tend to forget the obvious: every married person was initially celibate. And sometimes we minimize the fact that the success of a marriage depends strongly on the status of the people entering marriage—on celibates. Can celibates discover themselves in the solitude of aloneness and in the communion of friendship before and in service of surrendering themselves in marriage? Can they find their identity so they can be maturely intimate? Are they ready to give and receive instead of taking and acquiescing?

Furthermore, celibacy, with its opportunities and problems, can make sense as a choice, partly because marriage is an alternative. Likewise, marriage makes less sense without the freedom to be celibate. In a sense, celibates who want to get married should not get married until they are already married. This is not to say that celibates should live together in genital intimacy before they get married. Sexual adjustment does not mean marital adjustment. It does mean that celibates should not marry legally and sacramentally until they are already living in the permanence of marital love. The marriage ceremony should be an affirmation and celebration of an already existing commitment of love. To say, however, that a ceremony is not needed runs the risk of denying one's social and sacred dimensions. Even though the two partners consecrate themselves primarily to each other, they always have social responsibilities.

An authentic celibate life means that a *person* primarily commits him/herself to maintaining and promoting a life of love alone and with others. An authentic marital life means that *two persons* primarily commit themselves to a life together in love. A vowed celibate is not primarily committed to a community with another, but to a community with others.

Marriage should be a couple's paramount value and the place where they primarily express their love and consequently find lasting meaning. Indeed, although a couple's main concern is for each other, their love helps them to open up to others. For example, children, who can be manifestations of and witness to their love, demand that their parents be more than just for each other. Marital love can also help the couple love others outside their family; by loving each other, they are liberated for others. Nevertheless, they often cannot be as free for others as celibates usually can be.

Unique to marital love is the permanent availability of a couple to each other to give and receive love. Celibate love does not include a day-to-day and lifelong living together. In celibate and/or communal living, there is not "one" for "me" as in marriage. Marriage primarily means "you-and-I," whereas celibacy primarily means "I-alone-for-others."

Sometimes celibates can harbor a "celibate fantasy of married life." A celibate woman might think that marriage can be a panacea that answers all her questions, solves all her problems, and purges all her loneliness. Or a celibate man might imagine that genital encounter will help him mature and live a fuller life. Marriage does not solve problems. The marital situation usually maintains or exacerbates celibate problems, and with immature people encourages fixation or regression rather than growth.

We have seen that marriage includes a kind of celibacy. "Celibate genitality" can apply to marriage because in a sense married persons are celibate in all ways except in one way: to his or her spouse. That is, a person authentically married lives with and has genital relations with only one person, not with humanity. A married person is also a celibate in being alone in solitude. In fact, healthy marital love necessitates celibacy—self-discovery in solitude—for self-surrender in love.

Loneliness is also an essential part of marital love. In a sense, a celibate should not get married to ameliorate or to escape from loneliness but to grow deeper in loneliness. The more in love a person is, the more he or she can experience healthy loneliness. Such loneliness is a necessary dynamic of growing in love. Without the yearning of loneliness and the discovery of solitude, love is taken for granted, gets lost, and can die. Such "marital celibacy" can help a person come into contact with the ground of existence which includes everyone, especially his/her spouse. Celibacy is the ground out of which marital love emerges.

CHAPTER II

The Sexual Person

Consider human sex as the condition of embodiment that defines a human being as primarily male or female. Embodiment means that we manifest ourselves, experience and behave, and are seen primarily as man or woman. Because we are embodied, we are sexual. Being embodied gives us the possibility and responsibility to be sexual.

As a man or a woman I manifest myself in a sexual way. When someone comments on my body, they comment on me. If someone treats me as a sex object or just a body, they insult and degrade me. When my body changes, I change. Simple as these facts are, they are often forgotten. We can forget that we *are* sexually embodied people.

Many western thinkers and teachers have assumed that the body is secondary to the soul, and that the latter—spirit, psyche, mind—is what is really human or primary. Such thinkers have spoken as if our bodies were mere containers for the "deeper" realities. We may want to understand this truth: "We are our bodies," but we have been led to see our bodies as vessels for the spirit, and although we ourselves know our bodies, we often lack the words to express our knowledge. Scientists, like some biologists and physicians, have helped us to think of our bodies primarily as objects—something to be observed, analyzed, treated, and used. Certainly, such people have helped us in important ways. But if we view our bodies as secondary or as objects, we find it hard to express, to enjoy, and to celebrate our (sexual) bodies and selves.

A woman's menstrual process, for instance, is not simply a physiological fact, but rather an experiential phenomenon. A woman experiences her menstrual cycle and usually does not give much thought to the physiological dynamics. But since she is her body, her cycle influences the way she experiences reality, as in changes in mood and attitude. This is not to imply that a woman is determined by her menstrual cycle, for to be sure, she has a choice in her attitude toward this experiential phenomenon. The point is that the menstrual process is not something that a woman merely possesses, but an experience of what she is.

Being embodied inserts us as men or women in time and space. In this sense, human experience is always situated and therefore limited by time, space, and sex. Along with sensory and motor modalities, embodiment roots and anchors us temporally, spatially, and sexually.

Embodiment also means that a person's sociality is in some way sexual. Embodiment makes us humanly manifest—accessible and available to others—as men or as women. To see, hear, touch, yearn for, think about, speak to, or relate in whatever way to another is an embodied and therefore a sexual act. We will see later that since we are essentially social beings, sexuality is never exclusively a private affair. Sexuality is a social reality, and sociality is sexual.

Technically sex indicates a relatively static dimension of personhood—establishing the conditions which allow for the differentiations of the sexes. Sex refers to the inheritance which gives a person the possibility of being sexual. Nature, however, is meaningless without nurture, and potentiality is senseless without learning. How one's sex is actualized is contingent on both inheritance and environment, and the actualization of sex is called *sexuality*.

Actually, "sex" per se does not exist. Real sex is alive sex or sexuality. We experience sex, have sex, make sex, express sex, and are sexual. As contrasted with sex, sexuality points to a more dynamic aspect of personhood, to the interaction of sex and gender. Thus, sexuality or how we are sexual is contingent on sex and just as much or more on how we learn to be male and female.

Femininity and masculinity are parts of sexuality. Consider femininity as the way a woman has learned to manifest her sex, or how a woman has learned certain sex roles within a particular culture— *learned* and sanctioned ways of being a woman. For instance, in some cultures being feminine is often associated with qualities like sensitivity, intuition, receptivity, emotionality, and nurturing. Likewise, masculinity is a mode of sexuality that a man learns in a particular culture, and in the United States this is often associated with qualities like aggression, rationality, competition, and strength. We will see, however, that in order to be healthy a woman must incorporate so-called masculine qualities and a man must realize so-called feminine qualities.

Thus, being male or female is considered to be both a function of inheritance and learning. How a person is sexual is determined by his or her potentialities, by the environment that promotes and hinders healthy sexuality, and by the person's attitudes. It must be emphasized that sex and sexuality are not merely biological entities, but the way a person embodies his or her psychosocial, spiritual, and aesthetic self.

An assumption based on clinical and empirical evidence is that both men and women are bisexual. Within every man there is a woman, and within every woman there is a man. Although the sexes are distinct, they are not separate. A phenomenology of sexual encounters indicates that a man and a woman experience something familiar and something foreign in each other—that one sex is the complement of the other. In Jungian terms, a man meets his hidden *anima* or a woman her *animus* in the other sex. Ideally, each sex should complement the other—with neither dominating.

Thus, sex and sexuality are matters of accent—the accent being on male or female. Being a woman means that a person who is female has male potential. It can be said that her femaleness is in the foreground and her maleness in the background. Likewise, being a man means that a person is a male who incorporates the female.

HUMAN PERSONHOOD

Our understanding of sexuality depends on our views of the structure and dynamics of human personhood. To explicate my basic assumptions, I propose that human beings experience reality in four fundamental ways and combinations thereof: physically, functionally, spiritually, and aesthetically.

The physical dimension of a person refers to the structures and dynamics of a person's physicality. Though none of us is ever exclusively physical, we act in certain ways when most of our energy is invested in the physical. In themselves, our bodies demand immediate satisfaction, and our existence is centered around pleasure—a reduction of tension and/or pain. When we are in bodily need, we want something here and now; postponement of satisfaction makes no sense. Since we are "a needy me," we can act impulsively, without thinking of self or others. When we try to exist in an exclusively physical way, we want our needs satisfied regardless of anything or anybody.

For instance, an infant is a bodily self who craves immediate satisfaction no matter what. We say that infants are narcissistic—that life is centered around them. When an adult acts this way, the adult manifests regressive behavior. For example, if we are desperately in need of food, we may lose any sense of respect for self and others and act impulsively to gain immediate satisfaction. Our bodily needs take over, and we act exclusively on the basis of need satisfaction. We may literally steal or scream for food.

Physical sex alone means that we act almost exclusively on the physical level and that most of our energy is invested in physical sexual satisfaction. When we focus on the physical dimension of sex, we see others (and ourselves) simply as sex objects, and therefore degrade both. We have this option to reduce sex to an almost completely physical process because part of our being is physical.

Our functional dimension refers to ego activities that are centered around task-oriented behavior, coping mechanisms, and rational activities in general. Functionality refers to the way we function or the means we take to achieve our goals. Being human means that we can cope rationally with situations—analyze a situation and decide how to act. Most of us can deal more or less rationally with our internal feelings and thoughts and with environmental pressures.

Being able to function normally means that we can cope with reality so that reality does not overwhelm us for any extended period of time. Functioning normally means that we maintain ourselves and have adequate control over our lives. When we invest most of our energy in our functional powers, we can usually operate successfully. A danger, however, is to be so objective and impersonal that we lack spontaneity and personal involvement. We may live from the neck up, and therefore, in a sense, be out of our minds.

Functional sex means that we are in rational objective control of sexuality. Although information about and analysis of sexuality can indirectly help to improve it, such study has little direct place in sexual experience. Sexual theory and technique should be in service of experience and should become spontaneous. Otherwise, we will seldom spontaneously give, receive, and let go for any extended period of time. Our objective control impedes love and transcendence—essential qualities of healthy sexual relations. Furthermore, taking a hyperrational attitude toward sexuality lends itself to exploitation and manipulation. We may become sexual rogues who seduce others in service of our own sexual satisfaction and, more basically, in service of our will to power. Being able to handle others sexually can give us a false sense of power and security.

Spirituality is considered in this context to be the art of maintaining and growing in good and transrational experiences. Our approach to the spiritual does not explicitly include theology, Sacred Scripture, or other such sources of revelation. Our perspective is natural in that it is based on human experience. This does not imply that "supernatural" or other sources are denied or judged meaningless; in fact, our approach is probably congruent with these and other perspectives. Nevertheless, our discipline is primarily phenomenological and psychospiritual.

Spiritual experiences incorporate qualities such as paradox, mystery, and transcendence. Unlike the "either-or" process of the functional ego, spiritual processes involve an experience of "both-and." Instead of dealing with clear and distinct ideas, as spiritual selves we revere and surrender to mystery—a clearly unclear and inexhaustibly accessible source of meaning and fulfillment. Transcendence does not mean that we go out of this world into a different world, but that we go deeper into the world where we experience the unity underlying the differentiations. Such spiritual experiences as compassion, wonder, contemplation, and love are neither irrational nor rational but are transrational.

If we try to deny our sexual dimension, we become spiritual prunes. We lack vitality and deny embodiment in an attempt to be pure spirits. We are mad because we ignore the fact that our spirit is always embodied. Or we may see the spiritual as not needing rational powers so that we might say, for example, that spiritual love will solve all problems. The fact is that love without the implementation of rationality is often useless. The ideal is for the ego powers to be motivated by and permeated with those of the spirit. The healthy person integrates the irrationality of the body, the rationality of the ego, and the transrationality of the spirit.

Healthy spiritual sex incorporates qualities and activities such as care, respect, gentleness, and, most importantly, love. Spirit deepens sex, and sex embodies spirit. Sex gives spirit concrete humanness, and spirit gives sex lasting vitality. We will see that in spiritual genital sex a person can experience the ecstatic unity of concrete sexuality and transcendent spirituality. Actually, healthy spirituality can never be sexless because spirituality is always in some way embodied and therefore sexual.

Too often, however, spirituality and sexuality are separated. We can repress or deny spirituality in sexual encounters. Or, instead of despiritualizing sexuality, we can desexualize spirituality. Some well-intentioned people who strive to live spiritual lives repress their sexuality, especially genital sexuality, or they consider genital sexuality only as a biological function and, as a consequence, degrade human personhood. To repress sexuality while promoting spirituality is similar to repressing spirituality while promoting sexuality. Both are unchaste. One approach tries to make persons purely rational spiritual beings, and the other makes them purely sexual rational beings. The point is that we are unities of the physical, the functional, and the spiritual.

The aesthetic dimension refers to the unity of the physical, rational, and spiritual. For example, art is a harmony of embodiment, technique, and lasting meaning. A painting has its canvas and paints, a certain technique, and meaning, that is, it is embodied, rational, and spiritual. When we say that a person is beautiful, we do not necessarily mean that a person is physically pretty or attractive, we mean, consciously or unconsciously, that a person lives in harmony. We are beautiful when we live the unity of embodiment, rationality, and spirituality. When we repress or dissociate any of these three dimensions, we become less beautiful and more or less mad and sad.

Aesthetic sex protects and promotes the unity of matter, technique, and spiritual meaning. The beauty of sex is experienced, and beauty is seen as sexual. Most spiritual (loving) sex is beautiful because of its sex or embodiment, its form or style, and its love or spiritual meaning. Thus, there is a close relation between spiritual and aesthetic sexuality. The difference lies in how strong an accent is put on the spiritual dimension of the sexual experience.

HEALTHY, GOOD, NORMAL, MAD, AND BAD SEXUALITY

So far we have seen that any mode of sexuality— primary, genital, or affective—can be primarily physical, functional, spiritual, or aesthetic. Before we begin our concrete investigation of sexuality, a few more criteria and assumptions should be made explicit, namely, healthy, good, normal, mad, and bad sexuality.

Healthy sexuality is congruent with human actualization to the fullest possible extent, without psychopathology. Instead of repression, fixation, regression, perversion, or disintegration, healthy persons exhibit growth in wholeness and promote the welfare of others. The essential dynamic in healthy sex is love without psychological pathology and immaturity. Healthy sex is good and beautiful because it engenders the appreciation and nourishment of whole beings—the physical, the functional, and the spiritual.

Another key distinction is *normal sexuality*. Normality means that we can maintain ourselves and cope with the everyday demands of reality. Normal persons have a grip on life, can satisfy basic needs (including sexual ones), and do not manifest pathological symptoms. Still, such people are not necessarily healthy; we can be normal without being either unhealthy or healthy. Prevention of psychopathology (abnormal madness) is part of being healthy but does not constitute total health. In normal sexuality, we can cope with and effectively satisfy our sexual needs. In reducing sexual tension, we maintain ourselves but do not necessarily promote healthy growth.

Madness means that a person is closed to significant and necessary experiences. And normal people, not only abnormal people, can alienate themselves from the necessary experiences for healthy and happy living, and therefore become mad. In *normal madness,* we function within the confines of normal society and do not manifest pathological symptoms, but nonetheless we are closed to realities necessary for healthy living. For instance, workaholics, whose ultimate concern is work and who therefore downplay other significant experiences such as love, play, and compassion are normal but more or less mad. We will see that many kinds of sexual activity fall into this category. For instance, genital activity that reduces tension but does not promote growth and wholeness may be normal and mad—neither unhealthy nor healthy.

Mad sex usually refers to sexual exploitation and manipulation of oneself and others for self-satisfaction. Mad sex lacks concern, respect, or care. Some mad sex, such as sexual perversions and offenses, is classically unhealthy, and other sexual behavior, though not judged to be abnormally mad or socially punishable, is normally mad. For instance, treating another simply as a sex object is normal and mad, but such a chauvinistic sex offender is never punished by imprisonment as is a child molester. Although abnormal and normal sex offenses are not the same, they do have similarities. (See chapter seven.)

Sexual behavior can also be considered in light of goodness and badness. In our psychospiritual framework, *goodness* refers to the promotion of live emergence and therefore whole growth. *Badness* refers to the violation or destruction of life emergence. Thus, some persons can be unhealthy but good. Neurotic persons, for example, do not have to be bad but can engage in good activities. Such neurotic persons, though fixated or repressing experiences, may conscientiously try to promote life emergence and are therefore good. Other neurotic persons, however, may intentionally and consistently violate life by exploitation and selfishness. And normal persons who are not unhealthy in the traditional sense can be bad. Although these individuals are adjusted and lack pathological signs and symptoms, they live badly.

A main difference between being mad and bad is the level of intention. Mad persons seldom consciously or intentionally promote madness, but often unconcious processes motivate them to madness. In contrast to mad persons, bad individuals are more consciously intentional and exercise more choice over their behavior. Nevertheless, mad persons can choose to be bad.

Truly healthy persons are at least implicitly good because they promote wholeness and consequently life emergence. To be sure, healthy persons are capable of and can perform bad acts, but basically their lives are good. Normal persons who lead consistently good lives are likely to be healthy.

Healthy sexual activity includes an integration of the sexual and spiritual. Sexuality focuses on embodiment and spirituality accents love. Sex can vitalize, concretize, and incarnate love, and love can deepen, transcend, and spiritualize sex. But people who bifurcate sexuality and spirituality identify themselves and others simply as sexual or spiritual beings, and therefore are unwhole people. And though exclusively physical sex may incorporate pleasurable satisfaction and temporary fulfillment, such sex has little joy, depth, and permanence because it fragments and reinforces an individual's periphery.

Love without sex becomes disembodied, dry, lifeless, and unreal. Sexless persons become either cerebral robots or untouchable spirits. This does mean that we must actualize genital sex with another or self, but that we must actualize primary and affective sex. The ideal is to experience, not simply talk about, the lived unity of spirituality and sexuality. The challenge is to embody or to manifest love, and this is primarily a sexual and spiritual task. Healthy and holy people witness to this unity of sexuality and spirituality.

When dealing with the health and nonhealth and the good and bad of behavior, it is important to distinguish between the psychological (and moral) normative evaluation of acts and the clinical (and pastoral) counseling of people. We will analyze the structure and dynamics of sexuality and its possible sense and nonsense in service of establishing guidelines and ideals. And in dialogue with this relatively "objective" approach, we will discuss possibilities of therapeutic care for individual persons.

It is necessary to (and impossible not to) make value judgments and to propose norms for oneself, community, and society. The crucial issue is what kind of values we hold and teach. For instance, promulgating popular psychological theories of affective expression and faddish views of intimacy may encourage people to strive for norms that are incongruent with their psychospiritual growth. We make a significant impact on others with our views on interpersonal relationships, affective expression, and sexuality. Though teaching differs from counseling, teaching, promoting, and witnessing have a significant influence on communal and individual welfare. Thus, we have the responsibility to foster healthy views about sexuality while also trying to care compassionately.

Difficulty and challenge emerge when we find ourselves between the processes of normative evaluation and of therapeutic counseling. For example, though I teach that homosexuality is not healthy, I may choose to be silent about a homosexual incident, or accept its significance in the context of on-going life, or point out its irrelevance as an indication of homosexual orientation because I would judge such a course of action to be best in my therapeutic relationship with this individual at this time in our relationship. This does not mean that I would change my evaluation; in fact, I might clearly tell the client my views and then proceed with helping the client live the best life he or she can.

To help others we must know our own assumptions, feelings, thoughts, and values about sexuality. We should know where we stand in our normative evaluation and how it relates to our public and private therapeutic transactions.

CHAPTER III

Primary Sexuality

Although we may assume that there are certain differences between men and women, such assumptions can be questioned. Are women necessarily illogical and emotional, weak and docile, more caring than sexual? Are men necessarily logical and nonemotional, tough and competitive, more sexual than caring? Or are men and women more alike than they are different?

It is common wisdom that the experience and behavior of men and women differ to some degree. Yet, how the sexes may differ from (or be similar to) each other is far from being clear and conclusive, and why sexual differences and similarities exist is also a subject for extensive discussion and study. Primary sexuality is proposed as a construct to account for the modes of sexual existence—how men and women are present to reality.

We propose that in each person a propensity exists to be primarily a man or a woman. This is not biological or structural determinism, but an affirmation that structural conditions serve as the infrastructure for environmental learning. Instead of being mutually exclusive, heredity and environment are interdependent. And because of bisexuality, emergence in one sexual direction always incorporates aspects of the other sex. While focusing on the nature and nurture of men and women, the following models are proposed to shed light on sexual differences and similarities. Rather than being absolute explanations of the sexes, these models are heuristically used to clarify and integrate much of the data from both the hereditary and environmental approaches to sexuality.

MALE AND FEMALE EXISTENCE

Based on phenomenological analyses, the proposal is that a woman's existence tends to be centered, whole, and caring, whereas a man's existence tends to be differentiated, compartmentalized, and task-oriented. Because of innate and environmental forces, a woman's existence moves toward wholeness and centralization. Her experiences more than a man's tend to intermingle and to seek an integral process. On the other hand, a man's experiences are more apt than a woman's to be differentiated and compartmentalized. Normally, a man expends more effort to achieve a unity of experiences, whereas a woman's experiences move more spontaneously toward a whole.

A woman is not as likely as a man to separate or differentiate her experiences, but is more likely to interweave them. For example, if a woman and man have argued throughout the day and have not reconciled themselves, the woman is usually less inclined than the man to be intimate that night. The man, however, can more easily differentiate his experiences—in this case, the tense day and the intimate encounter. A woman is not as inclined to dissociate her experiences—in this case, her tense day from her encounter. This is not to say that one of these approaches is better or best or that they are mutually exclusive, but that they should be understood, appreciated, and integrated.

A woman more often than a man will try to unify sex and

love. For instance, when a woman joins with another in genital sex, she usually asks for some sign of love. Although such a request can be linked to approval, a woman's integrative propensity may also encourage her to look for love in sex. To be sure, a woman can separate sex and love, but a man normally separates them more easily. Similarly, though a woman can be intimately involved with more than one man at a time, such multi-involvement is relatively rare. A man, however, can more easily live such separate lives. Think of a "family man" who seems to be a good husband and father and yet periodically engages a prostitute. A woman can also engage in such promiscuous activity, but she is less likely to do so. This difference in behavior can certainly be highly influenced by cultural conditioning and by other such factors, but it is not necessarily totally contingent on them.

A normal man, more easily and frequently than a woman, can differentiate and even dissociate his experiences. Man's differentiated mode of existence means that he tends to put various experiences in different categories; his propensity is to involve himself in one experience while putting others aside. And his task-oriented manner can pressure him, though not necessarily, to be more distant from and less intimate with the totality of his experiences. Rather than integrating his experiences, a man is more inclined to differentiate them.

For instance, a man may not be as likely as a woman to look for love in intimate relations, and he can more easily separate love and sex. Or think of how easy it is for a man to treat a woman as a sex object—almost exclusively in physical terms. He can dissociate her physical sexuality from the rest of her being—fragmenting the whole woman and making her physical dimension her totality. A woman too can see and treat a man as a sex object, but not as easily, because of environmental and existential conditions.

Since all people are bisexual, women can differentiate experiences and be task-oriented, and men can move toward centeredness and integration. In certain ways, a man should strive to be more like a woman, and a woman should strive to be more like a man. The ideal is for man and woman to complement each other. The man learns to integrate his experiences—to promote and actualize the *anima* within him, while the woman's challenge is to differentiate her experiences—to realize the *animus* within her.

The reasons more women than men enter fields such as elementary education and nursing may depend upon more than cultural factors. Aside from cultural programming and expectations, perhaps a woman's integrative and caring style lends itself to such professions. Certainly, this distinction is not absolutely valid. Some men may be called to teaching young children or to nursing, and women can, do, and should enter fields such as university teaching and medicine.

Another hypothesis is that women more than men may have less need to be "out in society" and may have a stronger propensity to be home-centered. This is *not* to imply or meant to reinforce the sexist myth that women should be sweet, docile, and inferior beings who stay complacently bored at home and who are not publicly effective. It only suggests that most women may be inclined to seek situations professionally and personally that call for a caring and centered presence.

Everyday situations can be considered in terms of these models. For instance, a woman's dwelling space may be of utmost importance to her. If so, the architecture, furnishings, art works, and the general structure and atmosphere of her home should be congruent with and enhance her female experience. Unfortunately, too many men have designed and imposed on women living conditions that are far less than optimum to suit a woman's life. For example, female community structures such as convents and dormitories are often linear, staid, and "masculine" rather than centered, dynamic, and "feminine." Perhaps a female architect would design a building for women differently from a man's conception.

In this context, we are always primarily or existentially sexual. We must embody and manifest ourselves as men or women so that when we try to deny our existential (primary) sexuality, we deny and violate our existence. A woman, for example, who tries to live while repressing her female and feminine qualities gives less than is possible. A man whose care is totally cerebral represses his affective self and consequently cheats himself and others.

Neither the male nor female mode of existence is superior; each is equal and essential. One without the other leads to a fragmented and impoverished life and culture. Men can realize their female and feminine dimensions in their male and masculine ways, and women can realize their male and masculine dimensions in their female and feminine ways. Each becomes whole but not the same, alike but not identical. Such an integration of both male-masculine and female-feminine presence is needed for authentic living.

All persons, including hermits, have had primary sexual relations. Infancy and childhood involve homo- and heterosocial experiences that have a significantly positive and/or negative influence. And most celibates have primary sex relations with adults of both sexes. Although the kind and number of such experiences vary, celibates experience primary sexuality with others in reality and/or fantasy.

In a certain sense, we can also experience primary sex in nature, in the fine and performing arts, in literature, values, dreams, animals, etc. The polar dynamics of maleness and masculinity, femaleness and femininity, are present in all areas of life. A cloistered monk can encounter culturally defined feminine influences in singing, praying to the Blessed Mother, and to a large degree in his selfless and centered mode of living. Or a religious sister can find her so-called "masculine" counterpart in her feminine way in teaching, nursing, administrating, praying to God the Father, along with her direct contacts with men. To clarify and expand more concretely, these models of primary sexuality will be investigated from our four perspectives of the physical, functional, spiritual, and aesthetic.

THE EXPERIENCE OF PRIMARY SEXUALITY

Experiences of primary sexuality in its physical dimension can be positive or negative. For instance, if we see our body or sex as inferior, we can easily feel and act inferior. And we can be programmed to believe that our bodies are to be used for certain purposes and should exclude others. For instance, a woman may see her body primarily as a means for childbearing, of pleasing men, and being useful to men. She can learn to treat her body only as an instrument that is used by other people, especially children and men. Or a woman may be trained to use her body as an ornament that constantly must be made to look attractive for male approval. These kinds of unconscious attitudes can encourage fixation, docility, self-minimization, resentment, and unhappiness.

Men also can be trained to take negative attitudes toward their bodies. A man, for instance, can have a body image that stresses superiority over women. Or a man with a small body may feel inferior because much of Western culture supports the idea that a man's body be large and powerful. Men, however, often feel freer than women to let their bodies get out of shape, and women feel forced to stay "attractive" when in public or on display. The value of such standards is questionable. Still, we should take care of our bodies and in doing so take care of ourselves. Since our bodies are expressions and parts of our whole beings, caring for our bodies is caring for ourselves. And how we care for our bodies influences the way we express ourselves as sexual beings.

One of the clearest negative approaches to primary sexuality occurs when we treat one another as sex objects. What happens is that we focus exclusively on another's body as if that person were simply "a body" or some being that has a body—"somebody." Evident is a lack of respect for the whole person and equally evident is the insult to that person. One who is treated as a sex object feels degraded and often resentful. Instead of being appreciated as a whole being, this person is simply seen as a body to be exploited or manipulated. But there is no such reality as "a body," only a spiritual body or an embodied spirit. This reification process, making a person a thing, excludes or at least minimizes the person's functional, aesthetic, and spiritual dimensions; consequently, the person is denied spirit and thereby dehumanized.

We have suggested that a man and a woman do, or at least can, function somewhat differently. In speaking of primary sexuality in its functional dimension, however, an important point is not so much what men and women do, but how they do it. For instance, both men and women can nurture and compete, but how they nurture and compete may differ. A househusband's experiences of, and the way he functions with, children and housework may differ from a housewife's experience and mode of functioning. Or a female physician may do as good or a better job than a man, but how she experiences her patients and how they experience her may differ somewhat from a male physician's approach.

With the exception of some biological processes, there are

few if any activities in themselves that are exclusively male or female. Both men and women can and should have the opportunity to function in almost any area. And ideally, both sexes should participate in many of the same activities in complementary ways. Injustice and problems occur when one sex feels superior, oppresses the other sex often to compensate for underlying inferiority, or strives to be the same as the other sex.

Women have been and are oppressed in career (functional) areas. Instead of being blocked from pursuing certain fields, perhaps women should be encouraged to be slightly different kinds of engineers, physicians, or mechanics. As mentioned previously, a female physician may treat and care differently than does a male physician. I would suggest that this difference is not entirely owing to cultural programming. Perhaps a woman's caring and centering posture can foster a different kind of medical practice from a man's differentiating and task-oriented disposition.

Social learning is often unfair. Women may learn to think of themselves as socially inferior, nonassertive, docile, or in service of men, and consequently exclude possibilities of personal and professional fulfillment. Such oppression can begin in early childhood. Consider children's books in which little boys who grow up to be men are often in the center of activity, whereas little girls who grow up to be women are more often on the fringe of the action. Or how often is a physician, an engineer, a mechanic, or a minister depicted as a woman? Or, if girls are shown in such so-called masculine roles, what is a girl's chance to pursue such fields? These kinds of cultural conditionings can impede primary sexual functioning.

A girl may undergo pressures that a boy seldom experiences. Some girls may have freedom in childhood to be aggressive and to do their own thing, but in adolescence they may be pressured to learn social skills in service of eventually finding a marital mate but at the expense of giving up their vocational goals. Instead of being encouraged to seek autonomous self-esteem that is contingent on self-worth and ability, female adolescents may come to believe that their self-esteem primarily depends on how well they please and support men.

Indeed, women have been treated unjustly. Too often women have been forced into situations and roles they did not choose and have been banned from certain other places and roles. Not very long ago, a girl was seldom allowed to think about entering fields like engineering and medicine, simply because "women do not do this." Furthermore, men as well as many women thought that femininity and competition did not mix—that competition decreased femininity. The result was that a girl might abandon her vocational goals and sell herself short. Attitudes are changing, but there is still much prejudice against women in many areas.

Although the focus at present is on women's rights rather than on men's, men have also been oppressed and impeded from becoming wholly themselves. Many men have been culturally programmed to distrust their poetic and intuitive experiences and focus exclusively on task-oriented and competitive behavior. Their self-esteem too often depends upon career success. Many men have been programmed to see themselves as necessarily the only or at least the main economic provider and often the "head" of the home, church, and society.

A man may also question himself: Can I be truly affectionate with others? Must I function in so-called masculine ways that exclude spontaneity, gentleness, and care? Can I share responsibilities with a woman? Can I be a "househusband?" Can I surrender to a woman? How can women help me? Where is the woman in me?

The childhoods of various men also differ considerably and have a significant impact on their future lives. A man may question himself about his past. What were (and are) my parents like? Was my dad a "phantom father." Did he show affection and enjoy spending time with me? Was my mother overburdened with family responsibilities? How did she treat me? Did I always have to play with "boys'" toys like cars and guns, and did I have to play "rough" games? Did I learn to see girls as weak, passive, fickle, and servile or as domineering and cold? Was I taught that little boys do not cry and that they hide their pain? How do I see girls or women now? Is being a man the same as being tough and rough, or logical and competitive, or in control and unemotional? Do I feel free to express my whole self?

Men often think that the image of a man is much clearer and set than that of a woman. But what it means to be a true man is actually unclear. Is being an authentic man the same as being masculine? Since masculinity is highly influenced by cultural programming, what is masculine in one culture may not be masculine in another. Does a true man never cry, never feel intensely, never show his love? Is it "unmanly" to cook, to sew, to do housework?

A man can also be less certain of his identity because he is often much influenced by his mother and because he lacks contact with his father. Some fathers seem always to be working, golfing, bowling, reading, or just too busy or too tired to be available. If this has been true, a boy's early preparation for being a man may have been quite limited. Parenthetically, the absence of a mature man or father can also be detrimental to the growth of a woman.

Women may actually be more certain than men of their sexual identity. This may occur partly because mothers usually spend more time qualitatively and quantitatively with their children, and consequently present a role model for their daughters. Thus, a girl may have an easier time in becoming a woman than a boy has in becoming a man. Of course, a mother's attitudes are significant in influencing the kind of woman a girl will become.

Along with the physical and the functional, spirituality is also primarily sexual. Especially in western culture, however, there has been a strong tendency to consider sexuality and spirituality as mutually exclusive. Although sexuality has been despiritualized and spirituality has been de-sexualized, both sexuality and spirituality are integral dimensions of being a human being. A sexual—male or female—person is spiritual. To repress spirituality fragments the whole person, and to repress sexuality in service of pure spirituality is also a violation of authentic personhood. Fundamentally, we can only face God and others as men or women. Our avenue to spirituality is partly sexual. Spirituality without sexuality dehumanizes us. Healthy spirituality incorporates primary sexuality.

Our spiritual life can be influenced positively or negatively by the way we see ourselves as man or woman. One's personal history and cultural programming can have a negative impact on spiritual growth. If a man, for example, is subtly programmed to judge spiritual experiences as unimportant or secondary to achievement and success, he may be unlikely to promote his spiritual growth. Or if a woman is programmed to take a back seat in spiritual leadership, she can sell herself short or be limited in her contribution. She can docilely or resentfully accept a secondary role in religious matters. But are men necessarily more qualified or superior than women in these roles? Throughout history both men and women have been community leaders in spirituality and have written about spirituality, but women have seldom been in public positions of power and leadership. Is this necessarily the best way?

Other spiritual issues can be reconsidered in light of primary sexuality. Do men and women pray differently? Do they experience liturgy differently? Are meditation and contemplation different for men and women? Important differences that have seldom if ever been studied may exist. Such differences, however, would not be mutually exclusive but would embrace similarities because of bisexuality. For instance, when reading both male and female spiritual writers, one can explicate common and recurring themes. Still, there may be some differences owing to cultural and sexual forces. Perhaps men and women experience and articulate spirituality in different but complementary ways.

Perhaps harm may be done when only men establish structures and plan programs for women's spirituality. Men often direct and control, at least externally, the spiritual lives of women. This is not to infer that men cannot help women in their spiritual lives, but that women also can and should "officially" help women. And how often have women "directed" and helped men with their spiritual lives? Perhaps men can be hindered when they have access only to "male spirituality."

Consider some of the more functional, political, and ministerial aspects of religion. Think of how female ministry and leadership in religious and spiritual domains can be curtailed unnecessarily. A particular danger is to judge ministry only or primarily in male and masculine terms. Perhaps a woman could minister somewhat differently from and just as significantly as a man. Although women are "allowed" to promote spirituality and to have positions of authority in "their own" domains, they are blocked in many public positions of power and leadership—or they are "not taken too seriously."

A reason for such sexist religious oppression may be that women in leadership positions intimidate many men intellectually and sexually. Until recently, most men had more and better formal education than most women. Seldom was a nun as formally educated as a priest, but then many sisters and other women moved into higher education. Since they were kept out of traditional places of religious education like seminaries, women were forced to go to the universities. Consequently, these "naive, second-class" women often got as good or a better education than men. Furthermore, since many of these women were in a heterosocial university as contrasted with a homosocial seminary, they had more concrete and constructive opportunities to cope with celibate heterosexuality. Perhaps women's education, criticism, creativity, and heterosexual adjustment have threatened men to the point that they must keep women in second place.

Women are often used and patronized as workers in religious affairs, but seldom do they have positions of equality, authority, and opportunity. Ironically, though more women than men frequent and support places of worship, men still tend to want total or ultimate authority. What would happen if men shared their power and responsibility, listened to and learned from women, and worked and prayed equally together?

Love, the paramount dynamism of spirituality, can also be considered in light of primary sexuality. Do men and women love somewhat differently? It has been suggested that men may be able to separate love from other experiences more easily than do women and that a woman may have difficulty in being intimate with more than one man. Perhaps a woman is inclined to value and promote care more than competition, fulfillment more than success. Certainly, such differences can be culturally learned, and they can be negative when a woman becomes too dependent and lacks autonomy. Still, a woman's integral presence and tendency to promote love can be positive and powerful and need not be absolutely dependent on cultural programming. Unfortunately, too many women minimize or fail to use their own power in their struggle for political and social (masculine) power. Instead of proclaiming their own powerful presence, women can seek the questionable power of man and consequently affirm a false masculine superiority.

Perhaps man's propensity to be task-oriented has predisposed him to maximize the value of religious administration, of problem solving, and of rational theology at the expense of minimizing spirituality. Although men can talk about religion, they may feel relatively afraid or too weak to manifest and live the essence of religion—love.

Primary sexuality can also be considered aesthetically. A man or woman can be experienced as a dynamic unity of body, ego, and spirit. Here individuals are fully experienced as embodied persons, with functional forms and styles, and in depth—spiritually.

Who are beautifully sexual people? They may be very old, physically unattractive, or not functionally successful. Yet, they are beautiful because their spirit speaks and is in harmony with their embodied selves. Old persons can be sexually beautiful when they radiate dignity and wisdom. Crippled and deformed persons who are men and women of integrity are beautiful. Those who manifest the spirit of life and who promote harmonious and on-going wholeness are beautiful men and women.

An aesthetic experience of primary sexuality is similar to and differs from a spiritual experience because the experience of persons as dynamic wholes, an aesthetic perception, includes the spiritual. For example, artists and others who experience life aesthetically are at least implicitly in contact with the spiritual. The accent of beauty, however, is on the dynamic whole, while spirituality focuses on the spirit of that whole. Still, aesthetic experiences can foster spirituality and vice versa. It is not an accident that places of sacred worship often incorporate symbols of beauty. Objects such as paintings and activities such as singing can engender spiritual growth. Thus, a person who is closed to all aesthetic experiences risks impeding spiritual growth.

In summary, human beings, though bisexual, are primarily either men or women. This primary sexuality is experienced and manifested in bodily, functional, spiritual, and aesthetic ways and in combinations of these dimensions. Since men and women can be seriously hindered in being their full sexual selves, the ideal is to set the optimum conditions that promote healthy growth. The challenge is to strive to be wholly men and women—to be fully our sexual selves.

CHAPTER IV

Genital Sexuality

A common assumption is that celibacy should exclude genital feelings. To be sure, celibates are genital beings, and some believe that celibates must gratify, alone or with others, their genital needs; otherwise, celibates would necessarily be frustrated, "abnormal," pathetic, sick, or at least unfortunate. Indeed, although primary and affective sexuality are at least as important as genital sexuality, genitality can present more obvious problems for many celibate and married people. Still, people can be healthy without engaging in genital behavior, and genitality can promote integral growth in both celibate and married people.

Consider genital sexuality as behavior, thoughts, fantasies, desires, and feelings that involve or encourage genital behavior. In our approach to genital sexuality, a distinction is made between genitality and genital behavior. Sexual intercourse and masturbation, for example, are explicit forms of *genital behavior,* and feelings and fantasies that do or can activate genital processes are modes of *genitality.* Genitality incorporates genital thoughts and feelings that can but need not be actualized in personal or interpersonal genital behavior. Such signs as genital erection and lubrication and symptoms such as desires and fantasies indicate the activation of genital sex that may or may not be promoted or realized in genital behavior.

Paramount in our analysis is that genital sexuality in itself or as only a biological function does not experientially exist. Genital sexuality is an articulation of a whole person. When we try to identify with genital sex, we treat ourselves as less than we really are because genitality is one important manifestation, not the totality, of being a man or a woman. When we misuse or abuse genital sexuality, we misuse or abuse ourselves. And when we celebrate and realize genitality in a healthy way, we celebrate and actualize ourselves.

Also crucial to our presentation is that the processes of genitality point to transcendent goals and values. In genital relations, for instance, two people can go out to and receive each other in ways that go beyond them. Pleasure and pain, body and spirit, I and thou can find communion in genital love. The processes of genitality can also point to a third person. This is not to say that the only reason for genital intercourse is procreation but that a child is living proof that genitality transcends the couple. Children are manifestations of the basic process of genital transcendence, and any attempt to control this dynamism is an affirmation of its existence. Genital experience is transcendent in that genitality goes beyond the persons involved.

A simple fact, which is often forgotten or minimized, is that genital sex takes time and place. When we do not have or take the proper time for healthy genital sex, our experience is usually impeded. Rushed sex is usually far from what it can be. And if genital sexuality is constantly expressed quickly, it soon loses its vitality and spirit, for not having the time to unfold and to experience new meaning impedes healthy growth. Being embodied, we not only need sufficient time but also the right space to celebrate genital

sex. A genital encounter in an automobile can be an interesting change of pace, but as a frequent practice it becomes
more like genital gymnastics. The lack of a steady and comfortable home base eventually impedes genital relations.

When the time and space for good genital experience are
absent, tension and frustration eventually emerge
explicitly or implicitly. If nothing else such genital encounter becomes unwieldy. When we find ourselves planning genital relations, regulating the time, or hurrying the
experience, we soon become tense and frustrated. Being
discreet, changing places, or planning meetings can soon
become tiring and contrived. Constantly scheduling sex
militates against the rhythm and emergence of healthy
sexuality. Instead of becoming an integral and healthy part
of life, such behavior becomes too special and dissociated
from the rest of life. The dialectic between genitality and
other areas of living is violated, which can result in immediate satisfaction but eventual emptiness. Only a marital situation can offer the proper time and place for healthy
genitality to emerge. Indeed, marriage does not always pro-
vide the time and space, nor does it guarantee healthy sex,
but marriage is the situation within which healthy genital
relations can progressively occur.

The genital expression of love is a concrete and constant
reminder that the involved couple are more than they are.
Genital love is not only a pleasurable encounter but also a
transcendent mode of communication: the immediacy of
genitality is united with the transcendency of love. Genital
relations call on the couple to be responsible to each other
not for the moment, but for a lifetime. When a couple lacks
the commitment of marital love, its genital relations fail to
promote a permanent relationship. Genital love automatically calls for time, place, and commitment—which constitute a psychospiritual description of marriage.

MOTIVATIONS FOR GENITAL BEHAVIOR

We can engage in genital activity for many reasons, for genital behavior always makes some sense, and there is often much sense in apparent nonsense. The meaning, however, can vary on the continuums of healthy-mad and of good-bad which are highly a function of the motivation and situation.

The central motivating force in healthy genitality is love. Love incorporates a willingness to promote one's own and the other's welfare. Love is a good act because it encourages life emergence, and it is also healthy because it encourages integral and creative actualization. In genital love, there is a unity of sense and spirit, sex and love, sacred and profane. Genital love is a way of making the universal and transcendent immediate and concrete. Without love, genital sex can be unhealthy, but usually it is normally mad.

A common motivation for genital activity is satisfaction. We can engage in genital behavior to satisfy our needs and thereby reduce tension and experience pleasure. In genital climax, for instance, we are at ease, without tensions or needs, and feel moments of serene rest. We relax and breathe easily removed from the hassles of everyday living. Genital gratification is concrete, immediate, and stark, and its residue can last for hours and perhaps days. Nevertheless, its fulfillment in itself is temporary.

Acting only out of pleasure can be unhealthy, but it is more commonly not so—that is, it is normal. Physical sex can be more or less normally mad when we treat ourselves and each other simply as physical beings. Nevertheless, satisfaction and pleasure can and should be *parts* of healthy sexual relations.

Another possible motive is to escape or lessen painful feelings. Sexual gratification can reduce loneliness and be fulfilling. But when loveless genitality is used to escape the pain of loneliness, the fulfillment is temporary and the experience fails to promote the ongoing growth and commitment that are necessary for healthy relations. Although such sex is meaningful and understandable, it is not healthy or good.

Other feelings such as anxiety and depression can also be motivating forces for sexual engagement. Although genital satisfaction can lessen anxiety, such comfort should not be our main motivation. When depressed, sex may help us feel less empty and guilty and more loved, but these consequences are temporary so that later we may feel more depressed. A key distinction is not to use genitality only as a means of self-fulfillment and thereby use others in service of self.

To be sure, pleasurable satisfaction, comfort, and fulfillment can be consequences of loving genitality, but they should not be primary motivations. Instead, they are spontaneous consequences that can emerge out of a loving relationship and that can support and promote permanent rather than temporary relations. But when our motivations are primarily self-satisfaction, comfort, fulfillment, or other such reasons, we are usually normal but more or less mad. We are not healthy.

Ecstasy can also be a motivation for genital relations. Often we are able to forget or not be bothered by the tensions of everyday living while we engage in sexual intimacy. We can move out of our everyday world and into an erotic and comfortable genital world where the everyday dichotomies of pain and pleasure and I and you can come close to being one. When genital ecstasy is used primarily for self and as an escape from the everyday world, it is not healthy. Healthy loving genital relations, however, include ecstasy but as a consequence rather than a primary motivation. Mad ecstasy is separated from or an escape from everyday living rather than being linked with and a promotion of life.

A feeling of being whole can also be experienced in genital activity. Especially if we live a cerebral existence, a life from the neck up, genitality can be seductive as a way of affirming the rest of our being. For instance, a person who is a thinkaholic—one who operates cerebrally and sees truth only as emanating from the rational mind, may periodically crave to be whole and embodied. This person may engage in sex as a means of becoming whole and embodied. Though this makes sense, it is not necessarily good or healthy.

Similar to this feeling of wholeness is the striving for self-completion. In heterogenital relations, a man and a woman complement each other, a man finding his other half in a woman and she in him. In genital love we can become one with each other and can paradoxically become more ourselves. This kind of sex is healthy and actually promotes wholeness as well as bisexuality. Of course, if we use each other to affirm our weak or tenuous sense of sexual identity, our sexual union can be unhealthy or at least normally mad. This sexploitation may give us the illusion of being what we are not—mature persons.

Another seductive force of genital sexuality is that it makes us feel special. Persons who feel homogenized or who are caught up in the corporate structure of mass society may crave sexuality to affirm their uniqueness. (Persons, however, who are the most important realities in each other's life experience support, affirmation, and love. Their loving sex is special.) Even those who are exploited sexually may feel special, particularly if they feel senselessly lonely and worthless. Even though these persons know that genuine respect and care are absent, they may sometimes feel that anything or anybody is better than nothing or nobody. Unlike persons in love, exploited persons do not grow in the experiences of being special and later may feel less special or like "anybody."

In our nontouching society, genitality can be especially inviting because it moves toward touching in private areas. We get close to and unveil each other to some degree, and in this sense our behavior is beyond the routine. Instead of being distant, public, and cool, we are intimate, private, and warm—something special. Sex can be a touching experience.

Various power drives can also motivate us toward genital sex. The power of surrender and of being one with another in love is healthy. It is not the power of manipulation or exploitation, but the power of love—of being with and for each other. The power of pleasuring another can be healthy or mad depending on whether it is within love. The power of compensation, however, wherein we use each other to affirm our own sexual identity is normally or abnormally mad. This often happens to sexually weak people, and perhaps more frequently to men. Similarly, the power of conquering is usually mad because such power is contingent on feeling superior and is usually a compensation for inferiority.

Hostility, often in the guise of love, can also be a powerful motivation for genital relations. For instance, because of past hurt and present resentment, a woman can get back at a man, especially a chauvinist, by making him feel helpless in her arms. Or a woman can manipulate a man by using genital relations as a "reward" for expected behavior. A man who treats a woman as if she were a second-class citizen or a body to use for his own satisfaction can also be acting out of hostility. He sees a woman as an enemy— someone to use, lower, or hurt. Acting out of hostility is never good or healthy.

Past experiences can also motivate us toward mad sex. For example, a man who is highly dependent on his mother may spend time with women (or marry one) who are very similar to his mother and who mother him. He can be dependent upon them and expect them to nourish him, and perhaps fulfill his childish fantasies—to have genital relations with his mother. Or if he had been crucially hurt by a woman, he may have learned to hate and manipulate women. Likewise, a woman who idolizes her father may idolize men (or marry one) whose characters are similar to her father's. Or, if she were traumatized by a man, she might resent men and use sex to manipulate and dominate them.

Some of us may want to be genitally intimate because we have never experienced much intimacy with anyone on any level, including parents and friends. We try to transfer our fundamental need and desire to be loved into a desire to be genitally intimate. Genital satisfaction, however, is not an adequate replacement for the intimacy of love. Persons who experience the intimacy of love will have genital desires, but they are more likely to make sense of, to control creatively, and to integrate genitality.

The main reasons for any genital behavior centers around what we are searching for. A life focused entirely around immediate satisfaction leaves us restlessly empty and often means that we are unconsciously seeking more than pleasure. Often the implicit sense in mad and bad genitality is that we are looking for something more permanent. Senseless sex can be a search for spiritual sense.

THE EXPERIENCE OF GENITAL SEXUALITY

Our thesis has been that marriage is the vocational situation that affords the proper time, place, and commitment for healthy and good genital sex—sex relations that affirm and manifest love. Neither the religious nor the single life affords the kind of time, place, and commitment that can foster loving genital intercourse. In no way does marriage guarantee authentic genital intercourse, but it does set the conditions wherein such relations can occur.

We have also proposed that genitality calls for love—the central motivational force of spirituality. In open, gentle, and respectful genital love, two people can feel one with each other and simultaneously transcendent. Sharing without façades or pretense, we are not only purely present physically but also functionally, spiritually, and aesthetically. Love means that we are oriented to and for another—that we are willing to promote another's welfare for the other's sake. In genital love, two people can experience the communion of transcendent spirituality and concrete genitality. Genital love is a sacred experience that calls for wholeness and holiness.

Spiritual genitality can be and is experienced. Although there can be experiences that are almost totally or primarily a communion of spirituality and genitality, more often we experience moments of affective union, as for example, in a touch, a caress, a kiss. A complete surrender and giving in genital sex can also be an articulation of spirituality. When the accent is on spirituality within a genital context, we experience spiritual genitality. Perhaps more often, however, the physical and /or the aesthetic dimensions are accented within the context of love.

Genital relations can also be beautiful. Genital love is an art that involves a harmony of body and spirit within a certain form or context. Aesthetic genitality means that we are respected, appreciated, and embraced as whole persons. Regardless of their physical appearance, authentic genital lovers are beautiful because they give wholly of themselves.

Functional genital behavior can mean that we calculate, think, or manipulate during genital relations. For example, we may be efficient with the latest sex techniques, but still fail to be spontaneous. Instead of surrendering, we try to manipulate sex rationally. Although as sexual technocrats we may know all the techniques for sexual pleasure, we really do not engage and surrender ourselves. We are more likely to hide behind techniques and fail to give our whole beings in healthy genital relations.

Conscious technique and analytical thinking are primarily for the study, not for the bedroom. The more we control or manipulate a genital relationship, the more we lose the experience. Although there are moments of thinking in genital relations, too much thinking and technique violate the experience. Basically, rational approaches should be in service of experience, in this case, genital love.

Nevertheless, we have seen that functionality can and does play an important role in healthy sexual relations, particularly in aesthetic sex. The study of sex and the knowledge of various techniques can improve one's style and open new possibilities for sexual enjoyment. A key factor is that such knowledge develop into spontaneous sex. Healthy sexual techniques are basically prereflective ways to implement care rather than calculated techniques to engender self-satisfaction. As novices, our sexual techniques may be somewhat calculated and conscious, but as we grow older in love we function spontaneously in service of love. Instead of being calculating and rational, we know each other spontaneously and transrationally.

Physical genitality can occur when genitality is separated from the whole person. Although exclusive genital behavior can be normal in satisfying basic needs, it is neither healthy nor good because we treat each other simply as physical beings, not as embodied psychospiritual beings. When we see only genitality or certain parts of another's body, the other is seen and treated as a sex object, often to be manipulated and exploited.

Mere physical genitality violates the dignity and integrity of human personhood. If we engage in such physical genitality, we usually feel used or less than we are. There is always some inner guilt or subtle feeling of emptiness, which is experienced for good reason since we only share part of ourselves. Not all physical sex, however, is bad or necessarily mad. In the context of a marital commitment, the accent can be on physical sex within the basic context of authentic love. Here the marital partners not only pleasure themselves but also pleasure each other. They take and receive but also give. Their physical fun and genital play are always in the context of authentic love and ultimately in service of each other.

Celibate people, religious or single, can engage in genital behavior that can make sense and nonsense. Such behavior may be normal in that it can reduce tension and afford pleasurable satisfaction, but it does not permanently achieve and can violate wholeness and holiness.

Premarital genital sex may make sense to us especially when we feel empty, lonely, and perhaps worthless. Perhaps at times like these any kind of relationship can seem better than none, and genital contact without love can be temporarily fulfilling. Emptiness returns, however, and celibate sex is neither good nor healthy because it does not promote committed and responsible living and integral growth. Although we can learn from such premarital experiences, our growth does not come from the experience itself, but from the attitude taken toward the experience. We may discover that though there is pleasure, satisfaction, and temporary completeness, we are only maintaining ourselves instead of moving forward.

Obviously there are many kinds of celibate genital behavior. Recreational genital sex between strangers differs considerably from sex between committed lovers. In the former situation, people are likely to use each other for mutual pleasure, and their sexual encounter may be similar to mutual masturbation. Committed lovers are beyond recreational sex and are unlikely to use each other. Still, ideally, they should abstain because they still do not have the proper time, place, and commitment to implement genitality in the best possible way.

It may be argued that two unmarried people who live together do have the time, place, and perhaps (temporary) commitment to have authentic genital relations. Such a relationship may indeed be meaningful, but it lacks the permanent commitment that genital behavior calls for. Although their situation is more convenient than that of persons who must smuggle sex, the lack of permanent commitment militates against healthy and good genital relations.

Another possibility may arise when celibates genuinely love each other and sincerely move toward genital love. For example, a celibate man and woman may be intimate friends and in this sense, lovers. If they engage in genitality, however, their relationship seeks a different kind of commitment, or it violates and breaks their friendship because they lack the time, space, and proper commitment necessary for spontaneous and healthy genital relations. Such celibate lovers eventually find their genital relations militating against their growing in love. Their love tells them to stop if they want to keep their friendship. Because of their love, celibate lovers can say no to the meaningful experience of genital love. Although they may dislike doing so, they know it is best for their friendship. Thus, genital relations between celibates in love can be meaningful, but they do not promote ongoing growth. Genitality without marital love can dissipate and eventually destroy friendship.

Recreational sex, genital relations for pleasure and without a spiritual commitment, can also make sense in that genital needs are satisfied and pleasure is evoked, but a more basic and subtle emptiness remains. When we are treated as genital objects instead of as whole beings, we consciously or unconsciously feel dehumanized. To separate genitality and love is to fragment personhood. Even if we consciously agree to a contract of recreational sex, we are nevertheless exploiting each other and degrading ourselves. We offer and manifest only part of what we are instead of being and sharing what we wholly are and can become.

Such loveless or exploitive sex can and perhaps just as frequently does happen within marriage. When partners have only "quickie sex" to satisfy genital needs, their sex is not good or healthy. Usually this means the man has a quick orgasm, using the woman as a sperm receptacle, and quickly falls asleep without regard for his wife. The woman usually has little enjoyment and feels used and abused. A woman who is so used often becomes "frigid" as a protest against her exploitive and barbarous husband, so that such a no to sexual surrender can be an authentic yes to her dignity. Although quick sex can be a meaningful change of pace, it should not be a basic pattern.

It can be said that all forms of authentic love, except that experienced in marriage, exclude genital relations. Authentic celibate lovers are freed from marital responsibilities and are free to perfect all modes of intimacy except genital behavior. Unlike married persons, celibate persons do not focus their love on one human being. This does not mean that a celibate cannot be intimate with another person, but that such intimacy does not take a marital and genital form.

Questions remain. What can celibates do with their genitality? And what can married persons do when genital behavior is not possible, feasible, or appropriate? What can both celibate and married persons (outside marriage) do when they are genitally desirous and/or have the opportunity to engage in genital behavior? Can genitality and spirituality be interrelated and encourage each other in celibacy? Our proposal is that there can be a spirituality of genitality and a genitality of spirituality in celibacy. Let us consider the sense and nonsense of celibate genitality.

CELIBATE GENITALITY

Although each of us varies in genital desire according to constitution, learning, situation, and stage and kind of development, all of us, including religious and lay celibates, experience genital sexuality. To be human is to be genital. We all yearn to some degree to be genitally intimate, and such desires can be frustrating and confusing when gratification is partial or absent. We begin to feel incomplete or as if we were missing something significant without genital intimacy. Wanting to be loved and to give love genitally is a natural experience.

To compound possible pain, genitality, more than any other kind of sexuality, has been dissociated from spirituality. For us to say, then, that genital sex is linked to and can even promote spirituality may sound strange, but it actually can. We will see how genitality and celibacy, in and out of marriage, can be interwoven to promote healthy growth, and we will look at the sense and nonsense of separating genitality and spirituality.

Defense Mechanisms

Consider defense mechanisms as processes by which we protect ourselves against unpleasant or anxious feelings that tend to expose an unacceptable part of ourselves. When we use defense mechanisms, we reject certain aspects of ourselves because admitting such experiences would evoke unacceptable pain. Defenses are usually unconscious in that we do not consciously or willfully choose to use them. Such defenses, however, rather than being instinctual or innate, are learned processes, and therefore can be un-learned.

Defense mechanisms are not rare. Some authorities think that everyone uses them at times, and others contend that defense mechanisms are necessary to survive. How frequently, why, and how we use them greatly influences how mad our life will be. Our challenge is to become aware of our defense mechanisms in order to be more open to experiences and have more freedom for positive living.

Defense mechanisms can be normally or abnormally mad. Defenses distort our perception of reality. The more we use them, the more is reality filtered and biased. Defense mechanisms close us to experiences and thereby decrease our freedom and creative control of life, and they impede personal and interpersonal communication so that we are apt not to understand ourselves and others as well as we should. Furthermore, defenses tend to be self-reinforcing. The more we use them, the easier it gets and the more difficult it is to change.

Defenses exact a price. We waste time and energy in non-productive and repetitious behavior—in trying to be what and who we really are not. Moreover, defenses are not only painful to ourselves, but are frequently irritating and harmful to others. When we use them, we are more likely to manipulate others to satisfy our needs and less likely to be sufficiently flexible and open to understand and care for others.

A primary reason for using defense mechanisms is to ward off anxiety that is the result of unacceptable experiences. For instance, we may defend ourselves against genital feelings because we become anxious, ashamed, depressed, or guilty when we feel sexual. Although immediate unpleasantness may be ameliorated, we eventually lose because we say no to an essential part of our personhood. Defense mechanisms are self-defeating. Although there may be an immediate gain in the suppression of anxiety, eventually we end up in worse pain.

Repression more than other defense mechanisms is our focus because repression is often used to ward off anxiety that is evoked by unacceptable sexuality and because repression is often the basis of and pervades many other defense mechanisms. Those of us who repress automatically try to exclude certain experiences from conscious awareness. We fool ourselves in two basic ways: in not being conscious of certain experiences and in not being consciously aware of being unaware. We still feel sexual but refuse to admit to the experience—and refuse to admit to not owning up to genital feelings. We pretend not to be pretending. Confusing? Yes. This is why persons who constantly repress live in a world of pretense or of make-believe.

Repression is for the most part an unconscious process. To choose freely and consciously is contradictory to the dynamics of repression. Think of a woman who represses sexuality, especially genitality. She does not consciously choose to run from herself, for her sexual repression is primarily an automatic process. Although she may have some uneasy moments of questioning her sexual self, seldom does she allow herself to give her genitality a thought. If her repression is bluntly pointed out to her, she is likely to feel threatened and consequently become even more defensive. She may innocently deny, anxiously withdraw, vehemently protest, or sincerely intellectualize the truth. Whatever she does, she does not accept and affirm her sexual self.

Why do we unconsciously and automatically expunge experiences from conscious and free awareness? Usually, we learn and relearn that certain experiences are "unacceptable," make no sense, or are bad in themselves, and consequently "no good person" would experience them. We learn early in life that to keep one's self-esteem or to be a "loved me," certain nascent experiences must be repressed. To admit such feelings would risk rejection from others or create guilt (self-rejection).

Consider the sexually repressed woman as a child. If her parents constantly repressed sex in her life, punishing any sexual expression or discussion, she may have learned to feel that her self-esteem depended on not being sexual and thus felt compelled to repress sexuality. When sex suddenly and strongly emerged in adolescence, she would have found herself poorly prepared to integrate it within herself. Perhaps also her later years were sexually repressive so that her violence was reinforced. This woman never had the opportunity or help to integrate her sexuality. She had learned to feel that being a good person included being non-sexual. Unknowingly, this woman's sexual repression could restrict her life and impede opportunities for growth. For instance, silent solitude, which is essential to healthy growth, might be minimized because the silence of solitude could facilitate listening to what she may not want to hear—in this case, her sexuality. If celibate, her life might be an attempt to justify an exclusion of all sexuality. And if married, she might consider sex as an unpleasant means to procreate children and as an intolerable duty.

Repression is costly. When we categorically reject a dynamic that is factually part of our makeup, we pay a price. Repression is a negative reinforcement: instead of expunging an experience, repression can increase its strength and its pressure for expression. And the ways we unconsciously cope with repressed sexual energy are usually not in service of health. For instance, we may become frustrated, irritable, and angry. Or we may automatically abstain from intimacy for fear of being sexually activated, and perhaps use chastity and celibacy to rationalize such avoidance. Or we might project or displace our own feelings by blaming others for being unchaste, or perhaps achieve some vicarious satisfaction and shaky self-reinforcement by becoming the community's or family's "sex censor."

Whatever happens, we simply waste ourselves in trying to be what we are not. We become exhausted from going against the grain of existence, and our freedom is curtailed and our lives violated. Actually, absolute repression of sexuality is unchaste because it is impure and disrespectful to self and others. Such repression denies human embodiment.

Many defenses are based on and are variations of repression. Still, it can be useful to consider others in relation to sexuality so we can be more aware of the possibilities of fooling ourselves.

Denial is a refusal to admit that certain facts or actions exist. In contrast to repression, denial often occurs in interpersonal and social situations rather than in intrapsychic processes and is often a rejection of obvious evidence. For example, a woman's dress may be blatantly suggestive to others and to herself, but a man may completely deny that reality. Or a person who has physical signs of genital stimulation may reject any suggestion that such signs exist. Some persons may simply deny obvious evidence that they infringe upon or violate their vows.

Thus, those of us who deny use rather primitive defense mechanisms because we staunchly refuse to admit clear evidence, despite the fact that others may be aware that such reality exists. For instance, a third person might easily see that two friends are moving toward genitality, but the two deny that such an occurrence is happening. And some people who repress are so adept at keeping everything unconscious that they have no need to deny sexuality. It can be said that repression is the perfect denial.

Rationalization is an irrational way of using rationality. We rationalize when we try to abstain from confronting the real issue and attempt to explain and justify the way we feel or behave with impersonal and socially acceptable reasons. Instead of taking responsibility for our acts, we try to minimize their possible effects or try to justify our actions. In reference to genitality, for instance, we might say that everyone has genital feelings, so why worry about them. We try to hide behind a general statement instead of confronting our genital impulses. Or we might say that everything works out in the long run anyhow, so why worry or think about it. Instead of denying genitality, we rationalize sexuality. Still, we probably repress some genitality in that we have little free and conscious awareness of sexual impulses.

People who rationalize genitality often try to minimize the possible or real effects of genitality. For instance, celibates who enter a heterosexual friendship and begin to move toward or engage in genital activity can rationalize their behavior. They might say that their genital relations are in service of love or an expression of true friendship. Consider, for example, the minister who counseled a lonely and sexually frustrated woman. During the initial session, he was understanding and touched her shoulder; during the second session, he embraced the woman as a demonstration of his care. During the third session, he held her longer and had her sit on his lap. When she questioned his activities, he said that his behavior was a true expression of friendship and that there was nothing wrong in love. Finally, their relationship culminated with undressing and genital fondling. When the woman began to move toward genital intercourse, the minister told her to kneel down, and he gave her a blessing. He said that though they may have gone a bit too far, their emotional expression was in service of love and friendship. He explained to her that since love is the essence of Christianity, their actions were good.

Such rationalization may seem ludicrous to outsiders; it certainly was not to this woman. And it was not easy for her to listen to the minister's sermons on love while he embraced her. The minister, in his rationalization, was trying to have his cake and eat it too. Even though such a person can be holy and good, at the same time he satisfies his genital needs vicariously or directly and then rationalizes his behavior.

Fantasy can either be a defense mechanism or it can be healthy if it promotes reality. When fantasy becomes more important than reality or replaces reality, it can be more or less mad. Consider, for instance, a man who has many genital fantasies, seldom approaches people in reality, and rarely makes healthy sense of his genitality. Although he feels inferior to women, his compulsive fantasies of overpowering women serve as a way of overcompensating for his poor sexual identity and self-esteem. Instead of just becoming fixated in such a fantasy or becoming guilty about it, this person should understand, learn from, and integrate his sexual fantasies.

A danger of any genital fantasy is that it can become isolated from the rest of one's life. Fantasies offer the illusion of intimate fulfillment without risk, responsibility, and limits—elements of real intimacy. And when we try to gain more meaning, satisfaction, and fulfillment from genital fantasies than from other sources of life, our fantasies can be symptoms of serious madness. Still, as we will see, even the most severe madness can make sense.

Insulation is a defense mechanism that can especially lend itself to coping with genitality. Insulation occurs when we protect ourselves against hurt and disappointment by not allowing ourselves to care very much. Such emotional blunting enables us to be uninvolved. Instead of being warm and approachable, we remain cool and detached to protect ourselves from emotional involvement, especially sexual involvement. Although we may not be stimulated genitally or put ourselves in situations where this may occur, we may pay a price for this by becoming cold and life-less.

When we insulate ourselves emotionally, we tend to live "from the neck up." Even though we may be cognitively competent in administration and adjustment, emotional expression is checked by our not allowing ourselves to care in a personal and intimate way. A serious consequence of insulation may be emotional atrophy and loss of the art of caring. In the attempt to defend against genitality, we may lose our spirituality. Because caring might activate some genital feelings, we insulate ourselves and therefore violate spirituality—love. Thus, both spirituality and genitality are numbed, and life becomes flat, apathetic, less challenging, and lacking in enthusiasm.

A similar technique that may be used to impede healthy sexuality is *isolation*. We can cut ourselves off from sexual situations that produce stress. To be sure, to withdraw freely from a situation can be healthy, but to be compelled to isolate ourselves from any sexually stimulating situation is not healthy. Isolation may involve removing ourselves physically from areas of sexual discomfort by withdrawing from or refusing to continue an activity that evokes anxiety. Some persons never become involved with the other sex because such involvement evokes sexual feelings. Thus, they control sexuality by avoiding situations that evoke such stimulation. Some celibates, for example, may seldom if ever have heterosocial contact because of a fear of being sexually stimulated. Or a married person may always be involved with the same sex (he with the boys and she with the girls) and be too busy and tired to encounter his/her spouse. Or if such persons do become involved in a heterosexual situation, they feel compelled to withdraw prematurely. Instead of facing and making sense of their sexual emergence, they isolate themselves.

Another way of using isolation is to dissociate equally

important but mutually exclusive values. For instance, the counseling minister who felt urged to embody his love could probably isolate his questionable activities from his Sunday sermons. He could preach pure love on Sunday morning and forget about it during the week. Or consider the teacher who preaches the evils of masturbation to his students but frequently masturbates himself. Actually, the real isolation occurs between their values and their activities. Instead of trying to integrate thoughts and feelings, they isolate each in separate camps. Perhaps men because of their differentiated mode of living can more easily than women isolate or dissociate thoughts, feelings, and various activities from one another. Thus, to dissociate convictions from actions may lend itself more to a masculine mode of madness than to a feminine one.

Regression as a way of dealing with genitality may be more common than it initially appears to be. Regression is a reversion to activities that were more appropriate at earlier stages of development. When a situation becomes too threatening or overwhelming, we may regress to a level where we feel we have little or no responsibility or to a time when we felt more secure. Consider celibates who move out of sexual repression to some form of expression. Some may turn back to an earlier stage of development or to a stage before they began to repress so that such celibates may behave in an adolescent manner in the sexual area, even though they are otherwise mature. Their behavior will have an adolescent flavor in such things as constant giggling, sophomoric kidding, and crude joking.

To be sure, married persons can regress as much or more than celibates. Married persons who are threatened by the demands, risks, and responsibilities of mature love may act like adolescents as a way of protecting themselves. Mere physical sex is often a regressive act that prevents the integration of sex and spirit. Or think of the forty-two-year-old

Don Juan who tries "to make" his twenty-year-old sec-
retaries or students. His regression is probably a desperate
attempt to compensate for a weak and immature sexual
identity.

When we can only act like adolescents in the sexual
realm, we may be dealing with our sexual emergence
through regression. We may regress because it allows us to
feel less responsible for our actions or perhaps feel freer in
such expression. One of the negative effects, however, is
that we fail to integrate our sexuality with the rest of our
life, and instead act irresponsibly and immaturely. Some
celibate communities, in dealing with sexuality, become
either highly intellectual or sophomoric which only reinforces fixation instead of growth.

Some regressive behavior, however, can be congruent
with health. For instance, giggling and kidding about sex
may be a pleasant return to the past, an entertaining way
to explore new regions, or a way to work through certain
areas. Regression in service of health, however, is a change
of pace or a temporary growth period rather than a constant
way of coping negatively with sex.

A clear defense against sexual emergence (though not to
those who use it) is *projection*. Projection is an attempt to
maintain our self-esteem and adequacy by blaming others
for our mistakes or by imputing to others our own unacceptable feelings and impulses. We project when we accuse
others of being promiscuous or sexual because we ourselves
feel that way. Instead of admitting to our own sexual feelings, we project our unacceptable sexuality onto others. We
may even accuse others of being unchaste and manipulative
in their intentions as a way of dealing with our own unchaste and manipulative propensities. This can be difficult
for the accused because often they do not know what is
occurring. When people are accused, they may begin to feel
guilty, and the guilty person may be made to look innocent.

We can violate our sexual celibacy by placing the blame on other people or events. Consider a woman who has repressed her genitality in the name of chastity and who goes to a party where she drinks. Later that evening, she engages in genital relations, and the next morning uses projection to place the blame on the alcohol or on the man or on both. The point is that she does not accept her own responsibility. This helps her to maintain her false picture of herself as chaste, and consequently feel some degree of self-esteem as a chaste person.

Displacement is another common defense mechanism which, however, tends to lend itself more to anger than to sexuality. Displacement means switching the expression of feelings from the eliciting person to some other less risky person or object. Instead of expressing anger toward our boss, we automatically express the anger toward our spouse or friend. Instead of expressing anger toward a parent, a child beats a dog. Still, displacement of sexuality can and does occur.

Consider those men who go to prostitutes for sexual gratification. Sometimes these persons may be displacing their sexual feelings. For instance, a man who is sexually stimulated by a woman may be afraid to express his sexuality to her or to himself; instead, he goes to a prostitute. Or, similarly, a woman who is sexually stimulated may deny her sexuality and displace her feelings in masturbatory activities. Although her masturbation satisfies her genitality in some way, she fails to integrate sexuality in a healthy way. We will see in our discussion of sublimation that some people can displace sexual frustration into other activities such as overeating and oversleeping. Instead of facing their sexuality, they displace the sexual energy in other activities that do not promote healthy growth.

Compensation can be a subtle mode of defense against sexuality. Compensation means overreacting to make up for real or imagined inadequacy. Some celibates do not marry because they feel sexually inadequate; instead they become semicelibates who frequently engage in genital behavior. Their genital conquests are overcompensations for their feelings of sexual inferiority. Actually, these so-called celibates gain a sense of tenuous sexual identity from their genital exploitations. Thus, they compensate for their lack of authentic sexuality by indulging in crass genitality. Such persons can be deceptive because on the surface they may look like sexually active or open people, but actually they feel very inferior and too afraid to surrender in loving genitality. Their compensation is a mask that covers and hides their whole selves rather than uncovering and sharing themselves.

In our culture, men are particularly prone to overcompensate for their lack of primary sexuality by engaging in genital promiscuity. Men are often programmed to be the vanguards of genitality and to feel that they can somehow find true identity in genital conquests. As we shall see, when men begin to have less energy or interest in genitality, their basic sexuality can be highly threatened. Some middle-aged men, for example, can be seen to regress to playboy activities to compensate for their lack of mature sexual identity.

Another subtle way of dealing with genitality is to use a *reaction formation*—to replace unacceptable urges (sexuality) with completely opposite behavior and oftentimes correspondingly intolerant attitudes. People who go to one extreme often feel the opposite way within themselves. For example, sexual prudes are often highly sexual. (And sexual rogues know that they only need to press the right button in sexual prudes for their sexuality to gush out.) People who are all too willing to condemn sexual activities and who eagerly volunteer to be community sex censors may get vicarious and often direct satisfaction from their censoring.

Thus, some reaction formations have the advantage of maintaining one's precarious and questionable self-concept of being chaste and at the same time getting unchaste satisfaction.

Some individuals may try to lead celibate lives because they are afraid to face their own genitality. Celibacy to them means to be nongenital, and they may vow celibacy as a way of coping with unacceptable genital feelings. Such dedicated celibacy can also have the support of the culture or at least of certain subcultures. Certainly, this does not mean that all vowed celibates employ reaction formations against genitality, but for a few this is a possibility.

Reaction formations can be used even more subtly. Some persons control unacceptable sexual feelings toward the other sex by becoming overinvolved with the same sex. Since their involvement may include genital feelings and transitory genital behavior, such persons usually identify themselves as quasi- or basic homosexuals. Actually, their pseudohomosexuality is an attempt to control their feelings toward the other sex. Thus by identifying themselves as homosexuals, they control their heterosexual feelings.

Undoing often occurs with people who tend to be perfectionistic, scrupulous, and prone to guilt. Consider scrupulous people who have sexual feelings or fantasies. First of all, such persons usually identify feelings with acts, that is, to feel sexual is the same as behaving sexually. Thus, the consequent guilt is intense and frequent. They may waste enormous amounts of time and energy in trying to undo guilt evoked by natural feelings. Furthermore, scrupulous persons feel compelled to confess or do penance by means of perfect ritual. They may feel compelled to say a set of prayers perfectly until they have absolutely cleaned their moral slate. Instead of helping them to face and integrate sexuality, their undoing only buries it. Soon the submerged sexuality emerges and the corresponding compulsive actions are triggered off again.

If people do violate sexuality, they should feel guilty, not so much because of transgressing a law but because of exploiting a person. Undoing usually centers around guilt incurred by breaking laws that are unrealistic and serve only self instead of life emergence. Such atonement is unauthentic because it tries to maintain a sexual stand that is not healthy. True atonement means that people become one with themselves and with one another—integrated.

We can even use the defense mechanism of *sympathism* to defend against sexuality. Sympathism is the term for trying to get others to feel sorry for us and to support us. For example, if a woman feels overwhelmed by sexual feelings or unconsciously feels helpless in dealing with them, she may try to run from sexual awareness by always complaining about her problems. She may try to get others to feel sorry for her in order to indulge herself in their sympathy and hide from sexual awareness. This can be a rather subtle defense because those who listen to her may feel that such a sick and suffering person has no sexual feelings or does not think of sexuality. Complainers, however, usually and quickly turn off others and are left to themselves and their sexuality. Then they may be compelled to become even sicker so that others will help them run from themselves.

Acting out is another defense mechanism that may not seem so defensive because it is actually a gratification of needs. Acting out refers to the process of dispelling and reducing pressure by acting in a disapproved manner. For instance, those who repress genitality may periodically go on sprees of sexual fantasy, pornographic reading, and masturbation. Some persons rarely gratify genitality but once or twice a year they act out interpersonally and/or alone. Such acting out seems to lessen genital tension and may even evoke guilt that temporarily controls genital behavior. In a sense, such persons get their genitality out of their systems until it builds up again. Acting out is not healthy because it centers around impulsive gratification that is often caused by compulsive building up of sexual tension rather than an ongoing integration of sexuality and spirituality.

Suppression

Suppression is another way to deal with genitality similar to but radically different from repression. Suppression is also the checking of an experience. But, suppression, unlike repression, incorporates conscious or free awareness of an experience that is kept from overt expression. Suppression is a no that is based on a more fundamental yes. When we suppress genitality, we first freely affirm genital feelings and decide not to encourage or act on them. We actually express sex to ourselves and decide not to behave overtly, to suppress the sexual energy. Instead of being an unfree and unconscious decision, suppression is a free and often conscious decision. Instead of being engaged in a world of pretense, we accept and affirm sexuality and freely choose to control overt genital expression. Instead of the self-rejection and negation of repression, suppression is the self-affirmation and free choice that promotes healthy living.

Ideally, we should express all experiences to ourselves, but not necessarily to others and not necessarily in order to act on them. When we feel genital we should admit and affirm the experience. Such acceptance of sexuality, instead of repression, gives us more alternatives for action. Immediately or at a later time, we may mortify, sublimate, or directly integrate our genital feelings.

Pure suppression—the simple suppression of thoughts and feelings—is another important alternative. For instance, pure suppression of genitality may be appropriate while studying, for part of studying is to be sufficiently disciplined to focus freely without disruptive experiences. The student or scholar may neither desire nor have the time to reflect on genital feelings; thus, sexuality is simply put in brackets. Or consider a person who wants to help another with a personal problem. To listen and understand, a consoling person must suspend personal thoughts and feelings; otherwise, such a person listens to self instead of to the other.

Sexual suppression may call for mortification—a no that is in the service of a yes. Mortification, which literally means "to make death," is healthy when it is in service of life. For instance, if we feel genitally toward another person, we may freely choose to mortify our feelings. We first say yes to or affirm the genital feelings, and then say no to or mortify genital gratification. Instead of withdrawing from ourself and the other, we reject or "kill" gratification but still remain present, along with the sexual feelings, to and for the other. Thus, we remain sexual, but freely refuse to engage in genital behavior. We might say: "Yes, I would like to be genitally intimate with you, but no because of my other values." Such mortification is painful, but it is a death that can promote a life of love.

Suppression and mortification call for discipline. Some persons equate discipline with rigidity or repression; on the contrary, discipline is the basis of freedom. Others may find discipline difficult because in childhood all their needs were usually satisfied and because the culture often encourages immediate satisfaction at the expense of true discipline. Without discipline, it is possible to achieve sexual license, but impossible to be sexually free.

Problems for self and others can emerge when moving from repression to suppression. During this transitional time, a person may express almost the opposite of the past repressive behavior. Consider a man who repressed genitality and now becomes consciously aware of sexuality, perhaps because of some experience with a man or a woman, a counseling situation, or through an emergence of his own sexuality in solitude. Whatever the cause, this man may suddenly find himself confronted with genital feelings and fantasies. Confused by his newly emergent genital self, he may feel urged to act. Instead of being defensive about sex, he may show apparent flexibility and vitality, wanting to talk or think about sex considerably, and feeling urged to act sexually. Since his friends and fellow workers are used to him being his old "sexless" self, his new sexual self may conflict with their expectations and cause consternation. Some of them may try to pressure him to be his old self by criticizing him, by asking him what is wrong, or by alienating him. Or they might encourage him to gratify his genital desires or steer him to situations where genital gratification can easily occur. They would help him more if they were patient, understanding, just, and without being permissive, available to help him during this transition period. And, as he moves out of repression, this person should strive to suppress his impulses as much as possible, to mortify, integrate, and sublimate them.

Sublimation

Sublimation, another stand toward oneself, literally means to raise or to elevate. Consider sublimation as redirecting energy from one activity to another that is judged to be culturally, socially, physically, functionally, aesthetically, or spiritually "higher" or better. Sublimation, like suppression, is an acceptance of feelings that we do not want to express in certain behavior because of a conflict in values. Rather than holding it in check as in suppression, we rechannel the energy into activity that is congruent with our values.

Sublimation is a frequently used and encouraged approach in dealing with genital desires. Instead of directly satisfying genital desires, we can invest genitality in activities that are congruent with and promote healthy and good living. This is necessary not only for celibates but also for married persons. Married persons cannot and should not satisfy themselves every time they feel genital. In fact, married persons may have to sublimate genitality as much as do celibates.

Still, sublimation can be mad. Sublimation can be based on a false (Cartesian) philosophy of personhood that separates body and spirit, genitality and spirituality. Or conversely, sublimation can be based on a vision that posits pleasure as the main motivating force in life so that all behavior is ultimately in service of pleasure. Such a sublimation theory can maximize genitality and minimize spirituality. Sublimation, however, *can* be healthy and necessary.

We can sublimate genitality by suppressing sexual feelings (which includes affirming and controlling them) and then freely choose to sublimate the energy in action that promotes healthy living. Perhaps more in the past than at present, one approach was to "get busy" especially in manual labor or athletics. Although this kind of simple sublimation can still be useful and helpful, there are other ways as well. Sometimes we can rechannel sexual energy into academic or administrative work, or sublimate it in aesthetic and creative activity. Sexual energy can also be used to vitalize and increase concern for others. When suppressed and invested in love, genitality can promote healthy relationships. Instead of withdrawing out of fear, we can have the courage to suppress and sublimate genitality while remaining in and promoting a relationship of love.

Sublimation is often spontaneous, for we cannot and should not always suppress and then consciously choose how to sublimate. Persons, celibate or married, who feel sexual impulses may automatically involve themselves in another kind of activity. Sublimation, however, can impede healthy growth if based primarily or exclusively on repression.

Pseudosublimation, as this latter form may be called, is a way to relieve feelings such as frustration and irritability that can come from repressed sexuality. For example, persons who repress genital feelings may overeat—that is, unconsciously rechannel sexual energy into eating, an activity that can also ameliorate sexual tension. Others may become overly paternal or maternal with persons such as children or patients. To sublimate sex in care for others can be healthy and good, but when based on repression, it risks exploitation even in the name of chastity and of religious life. Sometimes persons may simply vent sexual frustration by becoming irritable and angry. Such sublimation is "pseudo" because instead of elevating or improving us, it can militate against healthy growth.

Healthy sublimation is necessary because of the limitations of being human. Being situated in time and space, we must choose how and where to expend energy, that is, we cannot do all things simultaneously. We can choose to promote certain experiences. And when celibate or married persons are urged via genitality to behave in a manner that is contrary to healthy living, they can freely (or spontaneously) choose to sublimate the energy in better behavior. One way to practice celibate genitality is to sublimate genital energy in behavior that promotes celibate or married love.

Gratification

We can also satisfy genital needs directly, and this is tempting for many reasons. Especially if we are tense, lonely, or depressed, sexual satisfaction seems to take all this away. Instead of feeling like nothing or empty, we can feel like something, someone, somebody who is fulfilled. Sexual satisfaction has a lot to offer: it can purge pain and give us a feeling of comfort.

We can engage in genital behavior to reduce tension and to evoke pleasure. Acting only out of pleasure can be unhealthy, or more commonly, "not healthy"—that is, while perhaps "normal," it does not foster personal growth. This normal physical sex is more or less mad and bad because we then treat ourselves and each other simply as physical beings, and this violates our integrity. We treat each other as if we were only "genital beings." Instead of integrating our genitality, we identify ourselves as merely genital, and consequently lessen our dignity.

We have also seen that a common motivation for genital gratification is loneliness. We may engage in genital activity to escape the pain of our lonely emptiness, and though this is humanly understandable, it is not healthy or good. When genital gratification is used to escape loneliness, sex and love are used as means of self-satisfaction and consequently violate the healthy process of sex and love. The experience becomes self-centered and the other can be (sometimes unconsciously) manipulated. Although normal, sex is also mad when loneliness is its primary motivation.

An escape from other feelings such as anxiety and depression can also be a key motivating force for genital engagement. Genital activity can make us feel less anxious and more comfortable, less guilty and more affirmed, or less empty and more fulfilled. But such behavior can be an escape from ourselves and from an opportunity to affirm and grow in spiritual living. Certainly, sexual satisfaction can ameliorate depression, anxiety, and loneliness and be healthy. Such reduction of discomfort, however, is not the primary reason for sexual activity but is secondary or a consequence of the activity. To make such satisfaction one's primary gain can be normally mad.

Finally, we have seen that celibate life, unlike the marital life, does not offer the commitment, time, and place that are necessary to foster genital behavior. Since genital sexuality calls for marital commitment, celibates who engage in genital relations may eventually feel cheated, frustrated, tense, unfulfilled, or resentful when this promise of love is not kept. And to be sure, married persons who do not grow in the permanence of their commitment can feel just as hurt and empty. Such feelings poignantly say that genital sex without authentic marital love eventually dissipates and is not good.

Genital relations outside marriage (between celibates and/or married persons) can be considered "normal" in that such behavior is frequently practiced, socially accepted or tolerated, reduces tension, and affords pleasure. But, mores are not the same as morals. Celibate genital relations are not healthy (though not usually pathological) and are not good.

Although celibates in love may be sincerely moved toward genital love, genital behavior will violate the relationship because of the lack of commitment, time, and place that are necessary for spontaneous and healthy genitality. Celibate (including pre- and extramarital) genital behavior, though meaningful, remains unchaste because it militates against psychological and spiritual growth. If two celibates or married persons fall into an intimate friendship, they may yearn to share and affirm their love genitally. And if they deliberately enter into relationships that explicitly foster genital sex, more particularly if they act on their genital feelings, their fulfillment is temporary and does not promote a good and whole life. Since friendship does not incorporate a marital commitment, friendship and genital behavior are incongruent. Actually, genital behavior in friendship calls for a marital commitment, or it destroys the friendship.

Respectful Integration

Though suppression and sublimation are important and necessary, they are primarily psychological ways of coping with genitality rather than direct ways of integrating genitality and spirituality. To be sure, these psychological postures are congruent with and can foster integration, but their relation to spiritual growth tends to be indirect. And a danger of these approaches is to consider genital desires only in terms of physical needs that are to be suppressed or sublimated rather than repressed or satisfied. Genitality, however, can have infinitely more than just a physical meaning. It can have a more direct and positive influence on our psychological and spiritual life. Instead of seeing sex as an enemy or impediment, a deeper challenge for us is to experience sex as a friend and help in living a celibate or married life of love. Genitality can evoke and promote authentic integration.

Integration means to experience the whole from which the part emerges. Integrating genitality begins with experiencing genitality as a differentiation and a revelation of the whole person. Instead of taking genital feelings, fantasies, and behavior simply as physical functions, we can listen to them as (genital) articulations that say something about ourselves and others as integral people. Chaste people experience the whole person who is the basis of and is revealed in genitality.

Respect, which literally means to see again or to take a second look, is a key to integration. Respectful persons look (in love) at genital sex as a manifestation of a whole person. Their *creative seeing* enables them to accept the invitation to appreciate the deeper dimensions of self and others. Instead of dissociating genitality from personhood or seeing genitality merely as a biological function, we can experience sex as an invitation to wholeness.

Actually, genitality can be an invitation to respectful integration. Genitality is a rupture in everyday life that can break through the forgetfulness and busyness of normal living to help us respect and fully appreciate ourselves and others. Specifically, genitality says to us: "Stop and respect reality—take a second look at yourself and the other. Don't take people for granted." What we see, however, depends on our presence to reality.

For example, a male artist as artist is not likely to see a nude female as a genital partner; he is more likely to see her aesthetically. His aesthetic sense appreciates her whole being—physically, psychologically, and spiritually. And in respecting her wholeness, he presupposes and actualizes his integrity. Likewise, authentic celibate or married lovers are not apt to identify themselves or others merely as a physical part (breasts, hips, genitals) or a function (companion, friend, lover), but are more inclined to experience these parts and functions as expressions and affirmations of whole human beings. Their respect for the other's integrity simultaneously assumes and nourishes their own wholeness, which can appeal to the other to respond as a whole being. Such persons are chaste—without narcissism, manipulation, or exploitation. A chaste posture is pure—a respectful and integral presence to reality.

We can see that sexuality is a social process in that it incorporates or seeks another person in relation to oneself. The other may be present in extra psychic reality or in fantasy, or be missing—present in his or her absence. Important in our discussion is that the way we sexually relate to others is highly contingent on our self-respect. When we appreciate another's wholeness, we affirm and manifest our own wholeness, and a respectful awareness of the other's integrality presupposes and fosters our own integrity. And to experience our own sexuality as an articulation of our whole being increases the likelihood of seeing the wholeness in the sex of the other.

We have proposed that women often seek far more than physical satisfaction when they feel sexually. Women are usually more inclined to see genital sex in light of tenderness, affection, and care, and they tend to hear more clearly the call for a permanent commitment in genitality. Of course, men can also see the depth of genitality and consequently become more sensitive to and concerned for others.

But men, at least in western cultures, are more likely than women, though not always, to see genital desires in terms of simple satisfaction. When genital desires urge a man to "take a second look," what he experiences depends strongly on his attitude toward the other or same sex. For instance, if a man experiences a woman simply as an object for sexual satisfaction, he identifies her as only a sexual being, minimizes or denies her functionality and spirituality, and consequently can desire to use her for selfish satisfaction. Yet his genital desires could help him to appreciate her as a *person,* as beautiful, intelligent, resourceful, as a mystery to behold, etc.

Think of a man, celibate or married, who is genitally attracted to a woman's breasts. What does he experience? Does he see only or primarily breasts? If so, his experience is unchaste. It is not healthy or good because no such reality as breasts exists, but only *a person* with breasts. He dissociates or represses the psychological and especially the spiritual dimensions of the woman and of himself, and consequently treats her and himself as less than she and he really can be. He lacks respect for himself, and he can lose his integrity because he fails to appreciate sexuality (his and hers) as an expression of a whole person.

A healthy stance would be to experience the woman and himself not only physically but also psychologically and spiritually—to experience himself and her wholly. Instead of fragmenting her being by dissociating her breasts from her personhood or by maximizing the meaning of her physicality, he could look at her more realistically by respecting her breasts as expressions of her personhood, womanhood, femininity, beauty, life, nurturance, care, centeredness, etc., and more so he could allow her breasts to evoke an appreciation of her whole being. He is then likely to keep and foster his integrity—to relate as a whole human being. His sexuality remains celibate and chaste, and it helps him grow in wholeness—including spiritually.

Consider sexual fantasies in the light of respectful integration. For instance, a woman may discover herself thinking or dreaming about genital sex. What does she experience? Does she imagine making love without weight, smell, touch, taste—a senseless love? Does she see genitals apart from the person instead of the person with his genitals? How real is her sexual fantasy? Does she fantasize about making love as just one euphoric state—without limits, fears, and clumsiness? Does she want the pleasure of sex and the perfection of intimacy without the limits and responsibility of real, loving sex? Her fantasies and desire to make loving sex are natural, but she should try to keep in touch with the whole of reality.

It is important really to listen to and look at what her sexual fantasies are saying to her because they can reveal something about her and her relationships with people. What kind of person is she as contrasted with her everyday self? Is she an assertive and adventurous person in sexual fantasies but docile and timid in everyday life? How does she act in her fantasies in contrast with reality? What does she want? In time, this person can discover her limits— honestly and truthfully how far she can go in fantasy to discover herself and promote growth instead of becoming fixed in immaturity.

The ideal is to look at and listen to all sexual signals. This does not mean that we should try to arouse and encourage genital feelings and fantasies, but that we carefully examine spontaneous arousal and fantasies to try to understand them. Genital stirrings are more than a physical message, and fantasies reveal more to us than mere genitality. Respect enables us to be open to various worlds of meaning that are revealed in genitality. Because genitality is an articulation of a whole person, it can be an opportunity to learn from and about ourselves and become whole.

Amplification can sometimes be helpful in promoting respect and consequent integration. Amplification extends, deepens, and enriches fantasies, dreams, and reality. Instead of repressing, escaping, or gratifying genital demands, we can amplify them. Instead of shunning genital feelings, amplification draws us deeper into them. Amplification does not mean that we should willfully activate or encourage genital feelings. The crucial challenge is to respect genital impulses and to see them as parts of the whole, as expressions of a person. To look for the spiritual in the genital can also help to maintain the perspective of the whole. We can really see and hear the whole person in genital strivings. We can come to feel wholly at home with genitality and experience the spirituality of genitality.

A person should not see or experience just an erect penis. There is no such experiential reality as "an erect penis," but only a person who has and is an erect penis. Likewise, there is no such experiential reality as "an erect clitoris," "erect nipples," or a "lubricated vagina," but only a person who has and is these sexual parts. To respect these sexual changes leads to integration—wholeness. Such sexual changes, for instance, can indicate that the whole person is standing out, moving toward, yearning for, and is receptive to intimacy with another. These sexual articulations can mean that a person's whole sexual being, not just genital being, is striving for more meaning and fulfillment. Genital expression can be one of the purest ways of uncovering the transcendent depths of being human.

Whether celibate or married, we can affirm and be grateful for such human emergence and capacity. Even though it can be painfully difficult to say no to genital behavior, we can actualize other forms of intimacy that genitality may be pointing to. Love, the spirit of life, can be discovered everywhere. Instead of covering love, genitality can uncover it.

But we can refuse the call of integration and focus exclusively on the physicality of genitality. We have seen that if this happens, we can experience immediate pleasure but lack permanent growth in wholeness. We further superficiality rather than depth. Failing to respect and promote the whole of reality, especially the reality of ourselves, we impede psychological and spiritual growth.

And too many of us, including religious, neither believe in ourselves nor trust our spirituality, and consequently we dissociate rather than integrate our genital sexuality. Instead of witnessing to the unity of love and sex, we can fragment and/or totalize genitality.

Healthy amplification incorporates a corresponding creative control. Instead of automatically satisfying, repressing, or blindly restricting our fantasies and feelings, we can discipline ourselves to follow the truth of our genitality. Our control is not based on violence—combating our genital self as an enemy—our creative control is a matter of being with—to approach our genital self as a friend. The relaxed discipline and attentive freedom of creative control enables us to test limits, expand horizons, and to deepen principles. Mad amplification involves stimulation or furthering of genital desires for immediate satisfaction rather than suppressing, mortifying, sublimating, or integrating.

Sometimes genital feelings can be so strong and loud that they tend to silence the messages of other feelings. For instance, a man may so yearn to be genitally intimate with a woman that he forgets other kinds of intimacy and loses creative control of himself. Consequently, he treats himself and her only as genital beings. *Creative listening* can help us to hear more than just genital messages. Perhaps such a person not only wants to be genitally intimate but also unconsciously seeks psychological, spiritual, and aesthetic intimacy. Perhaps within the nonsense of mere genitality is the sense of becoming whole with another. Perhaps within vice there is the struggle for virtue. Can we listen to the silent voice of spirituality in genitality?

Healthy amplification also means that we learn to face genitality (or any reality) openly and transcendently. Instead of seeing only a part or the surface of a person, we can be open to the other's integrity (wholeness) and experience the other's (and our own) dignity (worth). Such *creative* seeing cuts through the surface (transcend) to see and appreciate genitality as a manifestation of a whole person. To interpret genital yearnings only as biological drives, only as lustful needs, or only as "genital" is not only a closed perception but also a violation of the dignity of human personhood. Can genitality, celibate or marital, be seen in love? Can we contemplate genitality?

At times genital desires may not involve another person, but are simply present without an explicit other. Suppression or sublimation can be the most appropriate way of coping with such stark genital feelings. Still, we can integrate even these general or "a-social" sexual feelings. Once again, repression or gratification need not be our only choices but we can allow ourselves to unfold in genitality and to see where such spontaneous emergence leads our whole being.

Take, for example, a man who sees and is sexually attracted to a woman. He initially finds himself admiring and being aroused by her physical appearance. Instead of identifying her with her physicality, thinking of how "to make her," or repressing his vision, he can amplify his perception and thereby appreciate this woman (even though he never talks to her). For instance, he may look at the way she manifests herself—the way she moves and expresses herself, how she dresses and uses cosmetics, her body structure and her hair style—and wonder what this manifestation means to her as a person. What is she saying to herself and others? He may wonder how and why she shows herself in this way. What backstage activity is needed for her present action of herself? The quality, style, and color of her clothes say something about her life. Staying in shape does not usually happen accidentally. To look her best takes time and care. Such amplification can help this man become intimate with this woman even though she remains a stranger. Instead of taking a one-dimensional look, he sees her more deeply and wholly.

Consider a woman who has genital fantasies and feelings that center around genital intercourse with a man. Instead of stopping them prematurely, she can amplify her fantasies to see where they might lead her. For instance, instead of cutting off her fantasies at petting, genital play, or orgasms, she might speculate on what is likely to happen after sex. Do he and she suddenly disappear? Is everything all over and forgotten? Is there a future? If so, what kind? What real difference does such genital intimacy make? Will it make a person more mature? Better? Healthier? More loving? More committed? What are the real consequences likely to be?

Such healthy amplification involves an extension of the possible consequences of the fantasy and links it with reality. For instance, if the aforementioned woman could really experience her fantasy in reality, what would actually happen to her life? What concrete difference would such genital behavior really make? Furthermore, how would such behavior be likely to emerge or occur? Except in prostitution, heterogenital behavior usually does not suddenly appear and then disappear. Such amplification can be an affirmation of our embodiment in time and space and call forth responsible and committed attitudes and actions. Healthy amplification promotes respectful integration, whereas mad and bad amplification engenders the culture's madness—the separation of spirituality and sexuality.

Ideally, genital sexuality should help us become more alive and appreciative of the finer and deeper aspects of self and others. Genitality can be a pure proclamation of the dignity and integrity of being human. When we feel too afraid of or guilty about genital desires, we may see genitality only as a means of satisfaction or as something to overcontrol. Our goal is to respect genitality when it emerges so that whole persons can be seen and appreciated in and through it. This respectful integration is a chaste proclamation of the spirituality of genitality.

CHAPTER V

Affective Sexuality

We have seen that all human activity is existentially sexual. We work, play, converse, pray, or whatever we do as men or as women. For example, when a man and a woman engage each other, their primary sexuality partially influences the way they perceive, think, and express themselves. Some of our experiences have an overt affective tone, while others do not. A heterosexual interaction can also be influenced by an affective sexuality that embodies more feeling and emotion than does the primary. The woman, for instance, might docilely support the man to seduce him or she might clearly share her feelings, whereas the man might be affectively manipulative or be gently respectful. On the primary sexual level, their conversation is a cognitive, functional, and perceptual process, while on the affective level there are explicit affective influences that encourage or involve intimacy.

Affective sexuality refers to feelings, emotions, or moods that move toward or incorporate some form of intimacy. Such sexuality means that we are motivated to get close to another—to "touch" another affectively in a physical, functional, spiritual, or aesthetic way. This third mode of sexuality points to a personal and social relationship that involves or seeks closeness, or refers to the yearning for such a relationship.

Affective sexuality is a manifestation of and an invitation to be affectively intimate. The kind and degree of intimacy depend primarily on our relationships and motivations. Such intimacy may involve marital love, a close friendship, a gracious meeting, or a warm recognition. Furthermore, affective sexuality is one of many moves toward intimacy. Genital sexuality may more or less exclude affection, and though spiritual intimacy always includes primary sexuality, it need not actively or explicitly involve affective intimacy.

This point is significant: Affective sexual behavior can be an end in itself or can be in service of and part of genital behavior. For instance, a warm smile or a respectful caress can be ends in themselves, or they may lead to or be part of a genital encounter. Thus, affective sexuality can stand on its own as a way of relating to another person, or it can be a prelude to genital activity. When affective and genital sexuality are seen as identical or when affective sexuality is seen as leading to genital sex, unnecessary confusion and guilt can emerge. Consequently, some individuals might repress, unnecessarily suppress, or abuse affective sexuality—a healthy mode of sexual encounter.

Intention is the primary dynamic in determining whether affective sexuality is an end in itself or a means to genital behavior. A difficulty, however, is that we can be in conflict with our own intentionality and/or in conflict with another person. For instance, a man may consciously intend to be sexually affective but finds himself genitally aroused. His "thinking" and "feeling" are incongruent. Or a woman may be sexually affective with a man with no intent or experience of genitality, but a man may misinterpret her intentions and consequently encourage genital intimacy. Unknowingly, this woman may find herself in a situation she did not intend, and she may then choose to further or suppress genital involvement.

If affective sexuality does lead to genitality, we can then affirm the presence of genital sex and freely choose what course of action to take. A negative approach would be the repression of such genital arousal or the covering of these feelings with a veil of affective sexuality. The more open we are to the possibility of genital sex in affective encounters, the more we can creatively control genitality and choose whether or not to promote pure affective sexuality.

THE EXPERIENCE OF AFFECTIVE SEXUALITY

Affective sexuality can be clearly seen in its aesthetic dimension. "Affective aesthetic sexuality" is constituted of affective and aesthetic experiences so that feelings of intimacy are permeated with beauty—a harmony of the spiritual, physical, and functional. The whole person is manifested in a sexually beautifully way, and the person's affective move toward intimacy becomes aesthetic experience.

Consider a ballet that manifests eroticism and beauty. The performers demonstrate affective sexuality and show intimacy aesthetically. More than likely their erotic aesthetic dance is a means to genital sexuality. But if their dance were to be used as a prelude to genital intimacy, it would probably begin to take on a different tone and flavor.

On a more ordinary level, consider a man and a woman who dance with each other. Although their dancing may not be objectively aesthetic, they feel beautiful and they become affectively intimate as they dance. Their dancing can be an end in itself, or it can be an overture to genital relations. A married couple may dance in an erotic aesthetic way partly as a prelude to genitality, while two friends may enjoy their dance without such an intention.

Problems can emerge from the different motivations of partners. If a woman sees the dance as an end in itself but her partner interprets it as an invitation to genital sex, conflict arises. Using the dance as a means, the man will probably become genitally aroused or at least ready for such arousal. Frequently, a woman can sense his intention and consciously choose what to do. But if she is unaware of his arousal, she may be surprised when he becomes more explicit in his genital pursuit, and he may become frustrated and angry if his genital needs are not satisfied.

Another possibility is that a woman may misinterpret a man's intentions and think that dancing will lead to a date or spending a night together. But if the man has no such intentions, the woman may feel confused, hurt, frustrated, or angry when he leaves her. In either case, to prevent frustration, exploitation, or other pain, both partners should know their own and each other's intentions.

Still another possibility is that a couple becomes genitally stimulated unintentionally. If they deny such evidence, they are likely either to move toward direct or indirect satisfaction or feel frustrated and perhaps guilty. Or they might step back (physically, psychologically, or spiritually) and take stock of their situation. They can then decide whether to promote genital activation, suppress, sublimate, or integrate their feelings, or stop dancing.

There are also other forms of aesthetic affective sexuality. Certain psalms are a literary example. These poetic passages are spiritually centered—life in love—and are often affectively sexual. Such poems can be a prelude to genital intimacy or, without genitality, they can proclaim the joy of love.

Consider a man or woman who share and appreciate each other as whole beings. Their affection can include erotic feelings interwoven with aesthetic respect. Although such a relationship can lead to genital intimacy, it also can be an enjoyable experience in itself. Once again, however, when one who is involved is unaware of his/her own motivations and is not clear about the other's motivations, problems will result. Still, it is possible for a man and a woman to be chaste and celibate lovers.

Consider a man and a woman who share intimately. If one person intends this experience to be an end in itself and the other misinterprets it as a move toward more intimacy, problems arise. The man may interpret an affective aesthetic sexual encounter as a prelude to genital encounter, and if this does not happen, or if the woman refuses to enter genital relations, both the man and woman can be hurt. Or the woman may interpret this kind of experience as not in service of genitality but in service of a more complete and longer lasting relationship. A man may express himself in such an open and personal way that a woman might easily feel that he wants to further the relationship. Although his open care and true affection imply a future relationship, his intention does not include such a promise. The woman may want to see him again, but when he does not follow through, she becomes confused, frustrated, and perhaps angry. Ideally, the man should realize that his behavior could be misinterpreted and he should make his intentions clear; by the same token the woman should become more assertive and proclaim her feelings and intentions.

Similar problems can exist in marriage. One partner may want to be physically affectionate without entering into genital relations, while the other might misinterpret this affection as a prelude to genital encounter. For example, a woman may want to embrace and to be physically intimate, not as a prelude to genital encounter but as a way of expressing love. Her expression of affection is highly sexual though not explicitly genital, and too often the man misinterprets it as a desire for genital encounter. When the woman puts limits on or refuses genitality, both the man and the woman may become frustrated, hurt, and angry. It should be understood by both that all physical affection need not and should not lead to genitality. A couple who hold and caress each other may have an intimate, pleasurable, and loving experience that need not lead to genital sex.

Since the Western male is commonly seen as the initiator of genital sexuality a man can be oppressed if he is impeded from expressing himself affectively. And since our culture usually considers erotic-aesthetic behavior as feminine or sentimental, it may be assumed that although it is natural for a woman to be affectively aesthetic, it is not "manly." When a man expresses erotic-aesthetic behavior, as in the performing or fine arts, he is often considered effeminate or not sufficiently manly. Part of "being a man" is to be aggressive and controlled, but seldom aesthetic. For a man to be freely erotic-aesthetic he needs the support of a subculture such as a group of dancers or artists who will not criticize him negatively. Such criticism does violence to men because the erotic-aesthetic is part of a man's nature.

Men are programmed to minimize affective sexuality as an end in itself and to use it only as a means to genital sexuality. When a man expresses affection, he may feel pressured to enter genital relations. Thus, a celibate man may abstain from affective expression in order to avoid genital involvement. Or, as he grows older, he may minimize affection in order to avoid the "pressure to perform" genitally. To avoid embarrassment or guilt, the man simply constricts affective involvement.

For these and other reasons women have learned to suspect men or are confused by them. When a man expresses himself in an erotic-aesthetic manner, a woman will often hesitate and wonder what the man's true intentions are. As long as she hesitates or doubts the man, she cannot fully enter into the relationship. Yet her doubt is realistic because men frequently take advantage of a woman's trust. A man too often tries to "con" a woman on an affective level to "make" her on a genital level. Or the man may experience the woman as withdrawing from him, and if he has no intention of moving toward genital activity, he may be confused and consequently withdraw from her. Yet, if the man is using the situation as a prelude to genitality, her withdrawal may be wise. On the other hand, a woman may sense that a man can be intimidated by affection, and she may foster such anxiety to control or hurt him. Whatever the situation, aesthetic-affective relations should show care and foster mutual enjoyment and growth—not exploitation, pain, or selfishness.

Western woman tends to be evaluated primarily as the guardian of affective and especially affective-aesthetic sexuality. Thus, a woman is often oppressed in that she can be impeded from expressing herself genitally, though women have become more liberated in this way. Although a man may be more impeded and oppressed than a woman, such cultural programming prevents both sexes from being wholly themselves and from complementing each other.

Affective sexuality also can be primarily spiritual. Aesthetic and spiritual sexuality are similar and closely related, the key distinction being whether the aesthetic or spiritual dimension is accented. In spiritual-affective sexuality the accent is on spirituality with affective components. The style of some spiritual writers at times incorporates affective sexuality in contrast to a more cognitive approach. For example, the following passage deals with spirituality but is not affectively sexual: "A knowledge of God, which includes reading Scripture, is important in increasing one's spiritual life. If one does not reflect on the articulation of God, on God's Word, one loses an important source of spiritual data and motivation." Contrast such a passage with a more affectively sexual or erotic language that also focuses on spirituality. "My heart burns with love. I desire to be with you, and I yearn to give my all to you, O Lord, my Love. I want to embrace you with every fiber of my being and have you embrace me. Though I am unworthy, I am yours forever."

Interpersonal care is another mode of spiritual affection. In this kind of encounter, affection may be expressed silently or quietly as well as clearly and firmly. For instance, a warm and gentle smile can include some affective sexuality. Although the person feels the warmth of affection, the transaction is highly spiritual. The smile is mainly an expression of care and affirmation, but the affection behind it can be felt. Or consider a physical touch. When a son holds his father's arm or embraces him, affective sexuality can be present and remain in service of spiritual gratitude, or the two might touch each other in a way that includes respectful affection while focusing on love. Likewise, a compassionate person who confronts another may express affection in a masculine or feminine way. A conforting touch, a supportive caress, a compassionate word can incorporate feelings of intimacy. When the accent is on the spiritual, such behavior is unlikely to lead to genital arousal.

In contrast to aesthetic and spiritual-affective sexuality, affective sexuality can be primarily physical. Physical affection, which tends to be highly erotic and has no explicit spiritual or aesthetic influence, can easily evoke and lead to genital sexuality. Physical-affective sexuality is healthy and good when care is its ultimate motivation. For instance, a physical and pleasurable encounter between committed lovers can possibly be an end in itself, and can easily lead to genital encounter that is primarily pleasurable. Nevertheless, their ultimate orientation should be care for each other. Lovers can focus primarily on each other's bodies without treating each other as sex objects or persons to manipulate.

Genuine friends can also express physical-affective sexuality, though it can easily lead to genitality. The physical expression of affection can pressure them to share genitally especially when their care (or spirit) is more in the background than in the foreground. Behavior such as erotic dancing, sensuous touching, and sexually seductive language can engender genital arousal. If and when such stimulation occurs, then the friends can freely decide what they will do—promote, suppress, limit, stop, sublimate, or integrate genital sex. Friends ought to be careful—ready to show their spirit—if they engage in such erotic sexuality.

Physical-affective sexuality is mad or bad when no care is present or intended because the physical is separated from the functional and the spiritual. We treat each other as sex objects in order to satisfy physical needs alone. Once again, this dissociative process is not healthy or good because we are more than the physical. Think, for instance, of speech and flirtation that exclude respectful care, activities like dancing that focus entirely on the physical, or modes of dress that maximize eroticism and ignore good taste and style. These and other forms of physical affective sexuality can promote genitality without caring. If such affection does not culminate in genitality, frustration and anger can easily result because the implicit promise of genitality is not kept.

We can have different intentions in this area. For instance, a man can see a woman only in her physical dimension and respond in a physically affective way to pressure her into genitality. The woman may sense this and stop the transaction, or she may encourage it. A man or a woman may misinterpret physical-affective sexuality as an expression of caring and be seduced by it. Or a person's mode of behavior and dress may be intended to be aesthetically sexual, but be misinterpreted as an invitation to enter genital sexuality. Once again, it is important to know one's own and the other's intentions.

When the accent is on the functional, affective sexuality often centers around social behavior that involves qualities such as consideration and warmth. For instance, a man may behave like a gentleman and a woman like a lady when they show graceful consideration for others. Or they may display a sense of humor or tease each other in a light and easy way that can include affective sexuality. Although some clothing styles may be aesthetically or physically affective, many modes of dress are functionally affective. Clothing is a self-extension that indicates a way of living—and, style, color, and presentation delineate different life-styles.

Think of a woman in a social situation who expresses affective sexuality. Her behavior is neither explicitly spiritual nor primarily physical, and though it can be more or less aesthetic, the way she acts is mainly in service of a social and functional situation. She can be graceful and charming, warm and kind, considerate and friendly. Instead of being merely functional and thus task-oriented and highly cognitive, she also behaves affectively. She is a person of flesh and blood, not simply a cold functionary.

Consider a waiter who shows functional-affective sexuality. Although his work may be an art, his service is mainly a function. He can show a certain style, be socially gracious, and perhaps joke with his patrons. Without affective sexuality, he might easily behave like a robot or a cold functionary rather than a warmly functional person. Likewise, a waitress can express functional-affective sexuality by being warm and gracious and alert to her patrons' wants. She differs from the waitress who does not show any affective sexuality but is purely functional. Unfortunately, her affective sexuality can too often be misinterpreted as an overture to more intimate relations. Such sexist attitudes can curtail and oppress a woman's modes of expression.

Celibate affective sexuality should be an end in itself, not a means to promote genital sexuality. Affective sex in service of or as a part of genital sexuality can further healthy growth only in a marital situation, and marital affective sex can be appropriate as an end in itself. Furthermore, we have seen that we can and often should be affectively intimate in functional, spiritual, and aesthetic ways and that especially as celibates we can encounter problems when we indulge in or encourage erotic affection. It should be noted, however, that we do vary in our need and propensity for affective sex according to our sex, culture, ethnic group, temperament, environment, and stage of development. Our challenge is to find the place and live at the pace that promotes a life of (sexual and intimate) love.

CHAPTER VI

Celibate Love and Sexuality

Love has been proposed as the central dynamic of spirituality and of healthy and good sexuality. Without love, sex becomes mad and bad, and life loses its spirit and dies. To grasp concretely celibate love and sexuality, we will consider various forms of love in relation to the basic modes of sexuality. First let us reflect briefly on the fundamental structure and dynamics of healthy love.

Love is basically a transrational experience that transcends rationality and irrationality, the functional and the physical. Instead of being an expression of the periphery of existence as in the physical, love reveals the spirit of existence. And unlike the clear, analytical, and controlled processes of the functional, love incorporates the mysterious, paradoxical, and spontaneous. Rather than pleasuring or using persons to satisfy needs or working with or manipulating them to meet goals, people in love accept unconditionally, promote the other's welfare, and enjoy and inspire each other.

Love is the essential motivating force of a good life—the ongoing realization and integration of all that we can realistically be. Love gives us healthy and/or good lives because love is the spirit of life. Love is the breath that keeps us alive and happy.

Ideally, love is unconditional. For instance, if we only love when love is returned, our love is primarily self-centered, which is contrary to healthy love. Self-satisfaction should not be our primary motive, though it may be a consequence. Truly loving persons neither set conditions nor make any demands, for love is not a means to anything. Love is an end in itself.

Real love can be risky. Especially in its most intimate forms, love reveals and offers the most precious and vulnerable dimension of ourselves. Consequently, when we are hurt in love, we may be understandably reluctant to love again, but to expect never to be hurt in love is heaven, not earth. Although it can be extremely difficult, we have to strive to foster a willingness to suffer pain for the other's sake. Our painful love is not for ourselves, which is a form of selfishness or masochism, but "suffering love" means that we try *not* to withdraw, hurt in return, or play on another's guilt when hurt in love. Instead, we try to love no matter what happens.

In short, love is an invitation and an appeal to be wholly yourself and myself. In love I try to do what is best for you. I want to promote your well-being, and the best way is to love you and hope that you love, because loving is what is best for you. I love you for who you are, not for what you can do. I appreciate and respect you for what you are, not for what you have—your body, intelligence, skill, personality, background, wealth, reputation, or even your understanding, sensitivity, or love. I love you because you are you. In love, you are the one for whom I care.

Love includes many qualities such as care, concern, understanding, knowledge, appreciation, respect, and acceptance. And love can be expressed or embodied in many ways such as in marriage, friendship, or universal love. Our thesis is that behavior (including sexual activity) without love is more or less mad and/or bad.

CELIBATE LOVE

A major premise has been that healthy forms of love, except marriage, exclude genital behavior. Authentic celibate lovers are free from marital living and free to perfect all modes of intimacy except genital ones. As we have pointed out, celibates normally have more time and space to be alone and to be for others as contrasted with married persons who center more around one other. And some celibates vow to promote love of others and another—God.

Many opportunities exist for celibates to love through work. For instance, a teacher loves children; a nurse cares for people; an administrator tries to be just; a laborer does a good job for others; a social worker helps people; a cook nourishes people. These and other activities should be existentially sexual and can be more or less affectively sexual. (Such celibate love also applies to married persons, though somewhat differently.)

Daily personal life with others is another measure of love, and perhaps an opportunity more significant than work or with extra-community members. Religious in particular have the responsibility and opportunity to love community members. Healthy community living is maintaining and furthering common goals and values and growing older together in love. Such love should incorporate primary sexuality and can be affectively sexual.

Living alone is also a powerful test of love and sexuality. Although most celibates have friends and relatives, and religious also have a community, celibates more than married persons usually experience greater solitude and loneliness which can be painful but can also foster self-discovery and life appreciation. Because of their life-style and situation, celibates often have more opportunities to listen in solitude and loneliness than do married persons. This does not imply that celibates are recluses, but simply means that the daily experiences of celibates differ from those of married persons.

A celibate mode of living can increase the likelihood of experiencing transcendent values. Although celibates may lack the marital benefits of genital sex, children, and exclusive support, celibates find it more difficult to deceive themselves in their search for spiritual growth. For instance, their situation often encourages silence, and silence encourages listening. They usually have more time for recollection, contemplation, and similar experiences that promote love. Actually, authentic celibates ought to be the guardians and vanguards of love for others.

We have seen that marriage also includes a kind of quasi-celibacy in the sense that a married person lives with one person and has no genital intimacy except with that person. That is, married persons are celibates for all people except their spouses. Although this is a significant difference, married people also have experiences that celibates have. Furthermore, a healthy marriage includes solitude and loneliness, though perhaps not to the extent or in the same way as celibacy. Marital partners should respect each other's right and duty to encounter themselves in solitude.

Celibate love is always existentially sexual, for we must embody and manifest ourselves either as men or as women. When we try to deny our primary sexuality, our love is at least not as complete as it can be. A woman, for example, who loves while minimizing her worth and maximizing docility, gives less than is possible. Or a man whose caring is chauvinistic cheats himself and others.

From our psychospiritual perspective, genital behavior is not good or healthy for celibates, though it may be meaningful and normal. The celibate life-style does not incorporate the necessary conditions to enable genital sexuality to work in harmony with and to further a life of ongoing love. Nevertheless, celibates, like married people, have genital desires and needs. Let us, then, consider celibate heterosexual love—a love that usually incorporates affective sexuality and can lead to genitality.

HETEROSEXUAL LOVE

Intimate relations between the sexes expecially when one or both is a celibate can be problematic, mad, bad, good, or healthy. Can celibates be in love with each other in a healthy way? Can a married person be in love with a celibate or with another married person while promoting a healthy marriage? From an existential perspective, man-woman relations are necessary for healthy and holy growth. Since a woman evokes in a man and a man in a woman experiences that differ from monosocial relationships, men and women need each other to complement and fulfill each other. A man not only acts differently when with a woman, but he can also learn from her in ways that he cannot from a man. Likewise, a woman manifests herself differently when with a man and she can learn differently from the way she might in her homosocial relationships. Man without woman and woman without man fail to become whole persons.

Consider, for instance, a celibate man and woman dining together. Their experience can be a healthy way of enjoying each other. And if they regularly and privately dine together, their relationship can easily move from friendship to dating in service of more intimacy. A private and romantic atmosphere coupled with regularity can promote experiences that engender desires for genital intimacy. Such a man and woman can be honest and responsible with themselves and each other in understanding their possibilities and limits in various situations. Otherwise, "love games" in the name of friendship can emerge, or a promise of more intimacy may be implied but not kept.

In such a celibate heterosexual relationship, the man and woman can and should express their primary and affective sexuality. If they repress their affective sexuality, they may become cold and insipid. Although they may speak good lines, they lack the "touchability" and spirit of caring persons, and consequently their dining becomes boring and contrived. If the couple minimizes or represses spirituality, they may try to be only physical and/or functional—less than they really are.

When we accent and promote the erotic and exclude the spiritual component of affective sexuality, we can easily evoke genital desires that lead to frustration or satisfaction. For example, a heterosexual party can include healthy affective sexuality. A party, however, that stresses the erotic and represses the aesthetic and spiritual lends itself to finding a mate. More specifically: intimate physical dancing, erotic flirting, genital talk, touching games, and encouragement of erotic fantasy can generate the erotic-genital more than the erotic-aesthetic or more integral presence.

In short, all three modes of sexuality can manifest and promote love. But when we are not loving, we cover instead of uncover the whole person, and can violate and destroy instead of celebrating and nourishing ourselves. When we are open to both the opportunities and problems in ourselves, in others, and in situations, we can and should promote all kinds of love and sexuality except genital ones.

Vowed celibates can also love each other and be faithful to their commitment. Consider a religious brother and sister whose friendship periodically moves or seeks erotic and genital intimacy. They may express their love erotically in a loving glance or in a chaste touch, but they are careful that their eroticism be interwoven with aesthetic and spiritual qualities. In facing each other as whole persons, their erotic feelings are less likely to promote genitality. When their intimacy does evoke genitality, they set limits because of the absence of marital commitment and because of their love and religious commitments. They neither repress nor satisfy erotic and genital desires, but they affirm their desires and freely choose not to promote and realize them. And at times they may be very frustrated and dislike their no but they, perhaps reluctantly, freely put limits on the kind of sexual contact they share. Their no is based on a more fundamental yes—a yes to their desires, love, and primary commitment.

Religious and lay celibates along with married people can harbor false notions of chastity and celibacy especially in relation to heterosexual relationships. Chastity does not mean to be sexless, but to experience integrated and pure loving sex. Our love should foster growth in wholeness, not simply physical satisfaction or functional adjustment. Our challenge is to be maturely in touch with the endless possibilities of celibate heterosexual love.

Heterosexual intimacy can be especially problematic for people who have repressed sexuality or who are sexually immature. Consider a man who represses sexuality and suddenly enters a heterosexual relationship. Though he cares deeply, he may feel ripped with conflict, for his repressed sexual needs may strongly seek satisfaction. Erotic gratification can make him feel liberated and give him a sense of well-being that perhaps he never had, and feeling so accepted and at ease, he may find himself craving genital gratification. His difficult challenge is to promote his care and respect rather than be overwhelmed by genitality.

Or consider a woman who was sexually fixated in adolescence. Although she has not actively repressed sexuality, she is sexually immature in that she never had much opportunity to explore, understand, and integrate sex. If she becomes involved with a man, her experience may activate adult desires that her preadolescent attitudes fail to integrate. She could at times act like an adolescent, or she could become too dependent on the man and consequently minimize her autonomy. She could be a prime candidate for exploitation, or she could unconsciously exploit the man. Rather than becoming genitally involved, her challenge is to work through her psychosexual fixation with herself and perhaps with therapeutic help in order to discover and become her whole self. She may then choose freely how to give herself.

When we attempt to work through sexual fixation or repression while heterosexually involved, our sexual experiences can happen too quickly and intensely to be integrated. A common consequence is to feel guilty because our standards are incongruent with our experiences. Although we have new experiences (and often not at our own pace), our standards remain basically the same. We can feel the painful conflict between intense feeling on the one hand and equally intense belief on the other.

Some of us might say that we are guiltless because we have changed our standards. Invariably, however, we experience an inner guilt, not so much for abandoning standards but for not doing the best for ourselves and others. Our proclamation of guiltlessness can hide an underlying guilt that summons us to be and become our whole selves.

Even though we may be sincere and honest, we do not necessarily do what is best for ourselves and each other. Although honesty and sincerity can be ways to truth, this "honesty and sincerity" syndrome can be in the service of self-satisfaction instead of promoting the truth of love. For instance, we can sincerely and honestly exploit each other, or we can consciously be sincere and honest but unconsciously use each other. And we can hide selfish intentions

behind a façade of honesty and rationalize questionable behavior with a plea of sincerity.

We can strive to appreciate one another's values, standards, and psychospiritual development. Although certain
behavior may be healthy for oneself, it may be inappropriate or negative for another. Or both of us may be sexually
immature but in different ways. For instance, a man may be
overly aggressive and lose respect for a woman, while she
may minimize her worth and withdraw prematurely or
docilely submit.

Celibate heterosexual love can be more problematic for
married people than for celibates. Unlike celibates, married
persons have a commitment to another human being. Since
the marital vow of fidelity means that a couple pledge to
foster growing older together in love, extramarital genital
relations break their commitment to be faithful to each
other. Furthermore, such adulterous (celibate) relationships lack the time, place, and commitment that are necessary for healthy growth.

Still, extramarital heterosexuality can be healthy. A
married person can have loving friendships that include
primary and affective sexuality. But as with celibates,
when married persons regularly spend private time in a
relationship outside marriage, the relationship can easily
move to further intimacy. In addition, such married persons
take away time and energy from their main commitment,
which can militate against growth in their marriage.

Consider, for example, a woman who informs her husband that she is going to dine with a new male employee.
She may tell him that the man is a sincere and honest
person who is lonely and wants to know the city. She sincerely feels she must or should help him to feel at home, and
her husband may initially accept this situation, though he
may hesitate and feel ambivalent about it. But, if the

woman calls her husband a few nights later to inform him that the new employee is still lonely and therefore she must continue to help him feel accepted, her husband probably will become uncomfortable. He intuitively knows that such situations can easily lead to more intimacy. This does not mean that married persons cannot have friends outside their married relationship, but friendships, especially heterosexual ones, that are fostered in privacy can more easily lead to intimacy that militates against marital growth. Let us take a closer look at friendship.

FRIENDSHIP

Virtually everyone wants to have and to be a friend, and there are many reasons for this desire. There are some who search for "friends" to escape loneliness and boredom; while others may measure their personal success by the number of friends they have and feel guilty or ashamed if they have none; still others may withdraw from potential friendships because of fear or uncertainty. Some people feel that friendship is necessary to live a significantly meaningful life; while others are open to having friends but feel that they can be happy without intimate ones.

Friends ought to express their primary sexuality to each other and have freedom in affective sexuality. But painful problems can center around genital sexuality, and genitality can militate against a growing friendship. Before focusing on sexuality in friendship, let us briefly discuss what is meant by friendship.

Friends have a feeling of being at home with each other, experiencing a certain peace and enjoyment in being with each other. As friends we like and complement each other, and we like what we see and want to see more of what we like. And as this rapport grows, we promote each other's welfare. We can clearly face each other without conventional façades and protocols, for our relationship lacks gamesmanship, and if we do play games, we soon go beyond them. Our friendship includes mutual understanding and acceptance that give us a liberated and relaxed feeling. And our best friend is someone special—a person who comprehends the incomprehensible and accepts the unacceptable. No matter what, such a friend is present to and for us.

Friends can grow closer or grow apart because of their changing lives. For example, we can be the best of friends as young adults, and later separate and realize ourselves individually. We may renew and deepen our friendship when we meet again, but on the other hand, we can change and fall out of friendship. Although our past has an influence on our present development, our friendship is basically a precious experience of the past. Still, when we meet, we need not be negative, hostile, or strangers to each other. Though we are no longer friends, we can be friendly.

Furthermore, there are various degrees and kinds of friendship. While some friends grow closer throughout their lifetime, others are friends only at certain times in their lives. Some friends like to be with each other in any situation, while others prefer only particular situations. Friends may enjoy each other at work or at social gatherings (functional affective sexuality), or they may genuinely play together but not suffer together. All these friendships can be true and can involve various modes of sexuality. The friendship in which two persons can share everything with trust, dependability, respect, and fidelity is relatively rare. These friendships can sometimes evoke the most painful problems including sexual ones, and yet they can have the greatest rewards. More than three or four of these friendships is improbable. One is enough.

Friends are trustworthy and dependable. We do not have to worry about what a friend will think or do or that a friend will embarrass or betray us. With a friend, we can feel at ease in sharing because of the assurance of fidelity. In the love of friendship, we are willing to give to and help each other beyond the call of duty. We stand by, count on, support, and defend each other; we want to give more than what is normally expected. We are always available to each other, no matter what. Friends love each other. Like all love, authentic friendship is an end in itself; it needs no justification. As friends, we do not look for special gains or rewards, neither do we seek approval or a safe way of being liked or affirmed, nor is our friendship parasitic. We promote an unconditional and respectful concern for each other. Our friendship is chaste love.

Unchaste friendship involves exploitation. For example, a dependent man may satisfy another's need to rule and his own need to be dependent. Such a relationship is unchaste because it is primarily based on mutual need satisfaction, not primarily on giving to and supporting each other's welfare. Instead of promoting healthy growth, the two become fixated in a submissive-dominant relationship. Although unchaste friendships can be temporarily exciting and fulfilling, actually they are stagnant, closed, and temporary, not dynamic, open, and permanent.

In our best friendships, heterosocial or homosocial, we can be affectively intimate with each other. For example, a warm glance, an assuring touch, a respectful embrace can show our concern for each other. Sometimes we may authentically desire to realize our intimacy genitally—we want to give ourselves entirely, including genitally. And although genital relations might be an enjoyable expression of love, our intuition can tell us that genital experience would change our friendship and perhaps destroy it. We can come to realize that genital intercourse is one mode of intimate intercourse and that our celibate friendship can be just as intimate as a genital encounter. Although we may sometimes desire genital relations, we can freely, sometimes with painful reluctance, choose to say no to genital encounter and yes to our love.

In a certain sense, every deep and authentic friendship is particular. As friends we see each other unlike anyone else sees us, and we have and are something special. Such intimate friendships are especially available and fruitful for celibates. Although married people may have intimate friendships outside their marriage, a danger is that such friendship, especially heterosexual, militates against their marriage. Perhaps married persons should foster their particular and exclusive friendship within their marriage. In a sense, a married person's best friend should be his or her spouse.

ROMANTIC LOVE

Romantic love is in many ways the most exciting mode of love. It is the love of romantic writers, of youth, of those falling in love. It is the love that is embraced by all our senses; the love where there is nothing dull and mundane.

In romantic love, we feel intensely and often erotically, and along with the senuous and sexual we feel strongly involved with the ideal. As romantic lovers, we initially idealize each other, feeling that we can do and share anything and be our most perfect selves. We feel what love without limitations can be, and we want to give, to be, and to receive all that is possible. Our love can be so intense and total that it may feel like a fantasy which will disappear at any moment.

Romantic love can be experienced in many ways. For instance, without even falling in love with a particular person, young adults who are beginning to experience authentic love often idealize and romanticize love. Their experience can be healthy and good because it enables them to see what love can be. On the other hand, such persons may experience frustration and pain because honest and true caring is not always expressed in our culture. As authentic romantics, we may have particular difficulty in coping with people who manipulate and exploit or who are indifferent to the world of love.

Consider ourselves when we fall in love romantically. Initially we probably feel as though we are walking on clouds and that everything is possible. We experience each other in terms of perfection, hardly noticing our imperfections. We may feel that we want to live together forever and consequently get married. This romantic time of marital love is one of the most exciting, pleasurable, and fulfilling experiences of life. Enjoy and celebrate it.

Celibate friendships can have romantic periods especially at their starting point. As new friends we suddenly open up the world for each other in a new way. We may enable each other to feel that everything is possible and all is right. With each other, we experience life as radiantly alive, and we experience new possibilities for living. Our friendship may inspire us and help us come alive in a new way.

We can also have romantic experiences in solitude. For instance, we may feel intensely the spiritual possibilities of contemplation. We may experience a world of meaning that is transcendent and permanent. To ask ultimate questions and to be confronted with mysterious issues can be a peak experience. To hear silent music can be authentically romantic.

Romantic lovers—celibate, premarital, or married—initially experience each other's unlimited potential and celebrate each other's perfection. But this romantic period is usually followed by one of imperfection. Sometimes, suddenly, instead of experiencing each other as unlimited, we experience each other as very limited. We may begin to criticize, argue with, or perhaps withdraw from each other.

For instance, it is not uncommon to see an engaged

couple, who radiate love, begin to doubt their love shortly before or soon after their marriage. Instead of divinizing each other, they now demonize each other. This maximization of limits may occur several or more months after the honeymoon when certain patterns of behavior begin to irritate them. One squeezes the toothpaste from the middle and the other from the end. He may become irritated with and disapprove of the way she lives and she may criticize and reject his limits. Whatever the focus of criticism is, they notice each other's limits as contrasted with the past when they enjoyed each other's unlimitedness.

A different example is that of a vowed celibate who initially experiences the religious life as a perfect way of living. After this religious honeymoon, which often occurs during initial formation, this person may experience the imperfections of religious life. Community living may seem much different from the way it was in the novitiate or how it was described in literature. Living with others may be more of a burden than a joy. A danger is to identify religious life (or any life form) with its imperfections and obstacles to growth. The challenge is to grow imperfectly in the perfection of love.

This dialectic process can also occur in close friendships. Think of two celibates who care for each other and become close friends. Initially, they may idealize their relationship so that it becomes an exclusive one. At first, they may wonder how they ever lived without each other. Especially if one or both persons have repressed feelings of affection, now they can feel free to express themselves without restraint. They feel liberated and more wholly alive. (Genital involvement may be more likely during this time of perfection than at other times.) Their "particular" friendship, however, soon incorporates limits and obstacles. For instance, they discover that they can irritate and confuse each other, and they can become hurt, angry, and perhaps guilty and ashamed. Instead of withdrawing from the situation permanently, both persons can step back and listen to themselves and each other, and then return to renew and deepen their friendship so it includes both their positive and negative dimensions.

The ideal is that these two movements—divinization and demonization—be harmoniously integrated. In fact, these experiences point to and affirm what a human being is— both divine and demonic. We are always perfect and imperfect, and sometimes one of these dialectic poles is accented. When we experience a person as all perfect, it is helpful to keep in mind that every person is imperfect. When there are disagreements, past agreements can be remembered, and agreements that can come out of the disagreement can be striven for. The challenge is to see potential virtue where there is vice, potential pleasure where there is displeasure, joy where there is sadness, life where there is death.

To respect the rhythm of perfection and imperfection is helpful. For instance, romantic love, when erotic sexuality is stressed, can seduce us into thinking we are perfect and that we have no limits. We can feel "freer" for anything— including genital involvement. Everything except the other becomes secondary, and we may even demonize our past lives and divinize our heterosexual love.

Affective sex is a part of romantic love that is (and should be) particularly enjoyable. But a genuine desire to give one's self totally to another can present painful difficulties. Because of the affective and ideal qualities of romantic love, we may neither want nor perhaps experience any limits, and consequently may yearn to give unconditionally in every way possible. In our passionate and respectful love, we can forget that we lack the proper time, place, and commitment to foster ongoing growth. Though we would love to celebrate our love in genital experiences, we can say no (often painfully and reluctantly), but yes to our love.

Ideally, a radical decision or a life commitment should not be made in either the divine or demonic phases of love. When we are madly in love with each other and see no imperfections whatsoever, a life commitment is precarious. And we should be equally as prudent about making a radical decision while in a demonic phase. A practical principle is to make a crucial decision after we integrate the divine and demonic and experience ourselves and each other more wholly. If we are in conflict, we can try to wait until we make more sense of our struggle and feel freer to choose.

Ideally, we should not make a decision for life only out of romanticism or fantasy—when there are no limits or imperfections, but rather when we can be open to both the positive and negative factors of our past, present, and future situations. For instance, a man who falls in love with a woman may be in the divinizing stage of romantic love. When asked what is wrong with his beloved, he may say nothing concrete. Until he can point out experientially what is positive and negative about her and himself, it is probably better for him to wait awhile before making a radical decision to get married or remain celibate.

Authentic committed love is never all perfect or divine, and neither is it all imperfect or demonic. It is a combination of both. In fact, if authentic love were all perfect, commitment would not be necessary. Because we are a unity of perfection and imperfection, commitment is called for.

One reason romantic love is important is because it can be a prelude to a more committed love. Its strong attraction, gentle excitement, and erotic idealism make it easier, more enjoyable, and exciting for us to enter love. Love, especially intimate love, is a risky experience because we manifest and share ourselves most vulnerably and consequently can be crucially hurt. Romantic love makes the entry into love relatively easier, safer, and more fun. But romantic love is an intense promise of a more permanent love that is both ideal and limited, erotic and transcendent, for the moment and forever, pleasurable and painful, divine and demonic — a love that embraces and dignifies all of us.

This does not mean that romantic love is only a means toward an end. When immersed in romantic love, it is good to celebrate and proclaim our romantic stand to the world. Our experience is a witness to love and often promotes happiness for others. We also can create a precious source of memories that can be vitally present to us when going through difficult or easy times. And indeed as authentic lovers we can, though not constantly, consistently celebrate our love romantically.

DIVINE LOVE

Love is divine at least in the sense that when we love one another, our love is more than we are. In healthy love, we transcend everyday modes of behavior to the ground of our beings, to a reality related intimately to and beyond us. In love we can penetrate the mystery and spirit of being alive. We can experience a deep and lasting reality that never leaves us and that makes sense of all other experiences.

We love each other as sexual beings, as men and women. And divine love between human beings can easily include affective sexuality such as being gentle, kind, and sensitive. Both celibate and married persons can love divinely and be sexual in primary and affective ways. And, since it has been proposed that genitality calls for love and consequently calls for the divine, genital intercourse is sacred.

Love is also divine in solitude. Although physically alone, we can experience a transcendent reality that is the ground of existence and that is worthy of love and reverence. Transcending reality in divine love does not mean that we become disembodied or go out of the world; rather we go deeper into the world and experience the unity of differentiations—the whole underlying all differences. In the silent and serene simplicity of solitude, we can come to a knowledge of what life is ultimately about. In this situation we do not have to depend totally on others to experience love. Something can happen in solitude; a gift can be received that inspires us with more life.

Such divine love is also sexual. We listen, show, share, and surrender in solitude as men or women. We can also be affectively sexual in solitude by feeling intensely the divine grandeur and mystery that speaks of the divine encounter. We have mentioned that some spiritual literature is affectively sexual. Phrases like "naked intent," "enamored with the Lord's divinity," "a spontaneous desire springs suddenly toward God like spark from fire" are hardly asexual.[1] Prayer is often more or less affectively sexual. Making love to God and letting God penetrate us are sexual acts.

Divine love in solitude can also include genitality. When we experience genital desires, we can present ourselves as we are—more or less genital. To satisfy our genital desires could impede divine love because it could turn us in on ourselves, not toward God. But our genital desires can also manifest the power of love and creation, and can call forth the whole and point to the Holy. Genitality can be a yearning for the Spirit of Life. The end of genitality is love—the divine.

Although both modes of loving, with people and in solitude, should be actualized, one or the other can be accented. Depending upon such factors as background, temperament, personality, situation, and age, we may prefer one mode of love to another. For instance, one person may find love in solitude more meaningful, while another community member may like to love in direct dialogue with other people. Furthermore, how we love can vary through-

---

1. *The Cloud of Unknowing*, (Garden City, N.Y.: Image Books, 1973).

out life. At certain times in our lives, we may be more inclined to orient ourselves to other human beings, while at other times we may be more inclined to love in solitude. Both avenues of love, however, should be actualized because both are essential to a good and healthy life. When one of these modes is repressed or denied, the other begins to dissipate. For instance, if a religious sister (or any person) tries to reach the divine exclusively through human relationships, she can impede herself spiritually, as can a sister who excludes human presence. Still, we are free to accent one mode of love. As pointed out before, the celibate life, especially the religious life, lends itself more to love in solitude and with many others, and the marital vocation lends itself more to love with one other. In both situations, love is sacred—the ultimate concern that gives us eternal meaning. Actually, love is humanly divine—an imperfect growth into perfection. To love is to be divine, to dwell in the kingdom of God.

A LOVING DISPOSITION

A loving disposition refers to a readiness to love everyone and anyone anywhere and at any time as much as possible. Although we cannot be open to everyone at the same time, we can express love to people we see every day, once a year, or less. Such a loving orientation is normally expressed in day-to-day activities—in work, play, impromptu meetings, and social gatherings. Such behavior as thoughtfulness, respect, courtesy, compromise, genuine concern, understanding, and compassion can be manifestations of an everyday disposition to love. As with any mode of love, such love is existentially sexual and is often affectively sexual.

The disposition to love is our key force in good and healthy living. When the opportunity arises, we are ready to love in the best possible way. We are willing to promote another's welfare as best we can, which can mean being friendly, doing a favor, or withdrawing. For instance, to withdraw from another can sometimes be the best way to love that person. If saying something does more harm than good, perhaps staying out of a person's way for awhile is the best form of love. Sometimes giving nothing more than a friendly smile can be the best form of love.

Everyday love is seldom intense and intimate, and when it is, we should try to take responsibility for it. It can be unfair to share deeply and then suddenly leave or withdraw, for such intimacy can easily imply that more love is to come. An unfulfilled promise of more intimacy can breed pain and resentment. For example, Jane may be sincerely concerned about Joan who is lonely. In the name of love, she is initially willing to listen to Joan's frustrations and to help her realize herself in intimacy. But when Joan emerges in love and begins to seek a two-way friendship, Jane may suddenly set limits or withdraw. Jane, for positive and/or negative reasons, may be unwilling or unable to receive what Joan wants to give. Still, everyday love can lead to intimate friendship. When it does, rather than making implicit promises we do not intend to or cannot fulfill, we should be willing to take the time and effort to respond justly and authentically.

Everyday love, like any love or experience, is always expressed sexually—in being a man or a woman—and it can also include affective sexuality though usually not in its erotic dimension. Most everyday affective sexuality accents the functional and aesthetic dimensions. For instance, we can be gentle, considerate, and show a liveliness of spirit. The important point in our affective sexual behavior is that it be radiant with and emerge out of love.

It is usually good to know one another well before we begin to encourage directly the physical or the spiritual dimensions of affective sexuality. Otherwise, we can be intrusive or chauvinistic. For instance, after knowing a man for an hour, a woman may try to encounter him spiritually. If the man does not welcome this kind of direct care as he might in a counseling situation or with a friend, he could feel spiritually raped. Or to send physical signals that call for more intimacy can also be unfair. Sometimes we may immediately find ourselves at home with someone and feel it is safe to move closer without conventional preliminaries. This is not the normal process, but it can happen.

Although everyday love should not include genital encounter, it can evoke genital desires. For instance, a stranger can evoke genital feelings that will call for respectful integration—or genitality can be dissociated from love via repression of love or sex or both. The ideal is to allow affective and genital sexuality to be an invitation to appreciate the whole person.

To be good and happy, both celibate and married people should foster a loving disposition. This basic love, however, can in some ways be linked more closely with the celibate mode of living than with the married one. For instance, active religious are in a paradoxical situation of being open to solitude and to others. Not having a day-to-day commitment to a particular human being usually facilitates freedom for and commitment to others in and out of community.

CHASTITY

When speaking of love and sexuality, chastity must be discussed because chaste behavior includes the integration of love and sexuality. Unfortunately, chastity is often culturally interpreted as an impediment to or repression of sexuality. On the contrary, chastity promotes and nourishes healthy sexuality, for when sexuality is not chaste (integrated) it tends to be selfish and self-centered rather than being an opportunity for and an expression of respect and concern for others. Instead of promoting and being in harmony with love, unchaste sex is oriented around self-satisfaction.

Consider chastity in its basic sense as respectful and unconditional concern. As chaste persons, we act with respect: We take a second look at reality for deeper meaning. We take the initiative to look for more than surface meaning because we look at life with care. We do not experience one another only as physical beings because in love we see more than just the physical. To treat others only as functional beings is equally unchaste. And to see people as disembodied—only as spiritual—can be unchaste. To repress sexuality can be an unchaste act; to cut sexuality off from spirituality, or spirituality from sexuality, is unchaste. Chastity means to experience and to respect another as a whole person. Chastity is the virtue by which sexuality and spirituality are dynamically interrelated.

When we are chaste, we try to promote what is good because it is good, and we strive to give for the sake of giving. We do not act for what we can get from others, but we do what should be done because it is right. We behave with unconditional care, without the impurities of exploitation and manipulation.

Chastity means that we transcend such impurities as lust, manipulation, exploitation, selfishness, and pride. Acting only out of physical desire is unchaste because we treat ourselves and others only as physical beings. To manipulate another for self-satisfaction is also unchaste because it lacks unconditional concern and respect. Likewise, exploitation and patronization on any sexual level—primary, genital, or affective—is unchaste. For example, a man may be unchaste when he oppresses, pulls rank, or pities a woman, and a woman may be unchaste when she is masochistic, obsequious, or powerless. A woman is unchaste when she willfully castrates and frustrates a man, and a man is unchaste when he consciously asks to be mothered and controlled. Rather than manipulating or using one another, we can take care to respond integrally: physically, functionally, spiritually, and aesthetically.

Chastity also can help us to purge defense mechanisms that allow us to misinterpret reality. Repression of sexuality, for instance, is an offense against chastity, for repression of any kind of sexuality does not promote healthy integration. Simply because we do not behave sexually or indulge in genital relations does not mean that we are chaste. To minimize ourselves as men or women, rigidly to control affective sexuality, and to repress genital sexuality are modes of unchaste behavior. Some frigid, rigid, and sexless people may be the greatest offenders against chastity.

We can also violate chastity by being willess. We can give our will over to others and be willing to be formed any way others wish as long as our needs are satisfied. For example, we can violate chastity when we are too dependent on others for affection or sexual satisfaction. While sucking the life out of people, we will do anything as long as we are accepted, affirmed, and cared for. And we can invite and encourage exploitation, perhaps unconsciously. If we are passive and dependent persons, we can be unchaste in genital and affective sexuality and especially in primary sexuality. For instance, if a woman invites a man to dominate or manipulate her, she is being unchaste. Or if a woman allows a man to exploit her genitally (including in marriage), the woman along with the man is unchaste. To submit to any sexual exploitation can be a normal and mad mode of false chastity—behavior that violates and insults our integrity.

To be chaste, we must foster discipline and freedom. To be disciplined means to have creative control of life—to follow the truth as it emerges and to promote structures that engender self-actualization. In chastity we are constantly dedicated to making sense of impurities that may prevent us from being our best selves. We are careful of overestimating or underestimating the value of self and others. Interpersonally, we break through normal façades and games to be more available to others. Our freedom from the pollution of bias, egoism, and neediness frees us for love.

Unchaste sexual behavior means that the centripetal force of mere sex, especially genital sex, can impede or destroy the movement of unconditional care. Loveless sex is a violation of chastity that militates against healthy and integrated interpersonal relations. Such careless sex, however, is not the only violation of chastity. For example, our will to power, as evidenced in exploitation, is just as lethal to chastity as mere genital sexuality. When we do not truly respect and care for others, we violate chastity.

Some lay persons might think that vowed chastity and celibacy make no sense at all. We have seen, however, that chastity is necessary for healthy living and that celibacy is an option that can be healthy. Vowed chaste celibates can give witness to the culture, to the importance of chastity, and to the significance of celibacy.

Besides being explicitly unchaste, religious celibates can be unchaste in relatively subtle ways. Outside the community, a religious can exploit other people in the name of "chastity." For example, the counseling priest who somehow manages to counsel all the lonely, frustrated, and attractive women in his milieu may be unchaste. His concern for a woman's welfare may be a way of satisfying his own needs. To probe her inner life, especially her genital life, can satisfy his own needs and simultaneously give him a sense of being "holy." Instead of being holy, such countertransference is unchaste because it is primarily in service of self and secondarily in service of others.

Some lay persons think, however, that most vowed celibates break their vows or more or less "sneak sex" by having an affair or by masturbation. If not, then they think that religious must be repressed and frustrated. Indeed, rampant, secret sex does not occur, and though repression can be a problem, it is not a lethal epidemic. Actually, vowed celibates are probably at least as healthy in their sexual lives as lay people. It is unlikely that they are worse.

Most offenses against chastity are probably committed in marriage rather than out of it. For instance, consistent "quicky sex," wherein the man satisfies himself in a few minutes, is unchaste. As a change of pace, such sex can be chaste if it incorporates dignity, but too often it involves exploitation and selfishness. As a defense and protest against such sexual barbarism, a woman may become "frigid"—perhaps the only way she can say no to a man's unchaste behavior. A man is also unchaste when he pulls rank on his wife or takes her for granted. Men are often programmed to place women in roles that are in service of men. Their sexist expectations can be unchaste.

A married woman's unchaste sexual behavior may be more subtle. If she treats her husband like a son or another child, pulling sexual rank on him, even though he may unconsciously ask for such treatment she may be acting unchastely. If she is frequently flirtatious or suggestive and consistently withdraws from more intimacy, she may be unchaste. And she is probably unchaste if her affective sexuality is never in service of genital relations. Affective sexuality can and should be healthy and positive as an end in itself, but within the context of marriage it can also be a prelude to genital sexuality. A woman may also be unchaste in using genital sexuality to manipulate her husband. Instead of confronting him with the real issues, she punishes him by refusing to have genital relations. She is, in effect, making the following proposal: If you do what I say, then I will satisfy you. Both partners of such a contract are unchaste.

In many, although certainly not all ways, lay celibates may have the most difficult time practicing the virtue of chastity. Unlike married or religious persons, single persons usually do not have the support and affirmation of a consistent community. Especially when in the throes of loneliness, single persons can be under intense pressure to act unchastely because the immediate sexual fulfillment, though it is temporary, can be awfully tempting when one feels like nothing. We can, of course, separate love and sex and have a pleasurable and satisfying experience, but the healthy and often painful challenge is to promote chaste sex.

Single women especially may be treated unchastely, for many married and unmarried men are willing to exploit single women. A man can take advantage of a woman's loneliness or stimulate her sexual needs, and perhaps offer a caricature of caring. Of course, women can encourage such exploitation, or they can actively exploit. Recreational sex, when sex and love are separated, can be very tempting. But to indulge in such sex does not promote an integration of sexuality and spirituality, and therefore does not promote healthy growth. Although unchaste behavior may be normal, human, and meaningful, it is not healthy or good.

As chaste people, married or unmarried, we are direct, simple, and transparent. We are neither collusive nor deceptive. We show ourselves as we are and see others for what they are and can be. Sexuality is not simply something to cope with or a problem to solve and neither is it simply a source of satisfaction, but in chastity we see and celebrate the mystery—the spirit—of sex.

Chastity is a virtue that promotes a good and healthy life. Thus, both married and unmarried people ought to encourage chastity, and religious celibates should vow to keep and deepen the virtue of chastity. Although chastity does not have to include celibacy, the religious vow of chastity does incorporate celibacy. Religious vow chastity because chastity is necessary for a good and healthy life, and their chastity incorporates celibacy to give witness in community to spirituality.

CHAPTER VII

Sexual Madness

We have described madness as estrangement from experiences that are essential for healthy and happy living. Most psychotic persons, for whatever reasons, cannot function normally in the everyday world. But normal people, such as workaholics, can also be mad. Unlike psychotics, workaholics can cope, compete, and communicate, usually very well, but they probably repress, minimize, or forget significant experiences such as play and love. Although such normal people are not abnormally mad (psychotic), they are normally mad. In this chapter, we should like to look at some abnormal and normal modes of sexual madness. Much has been written about the madness of sexism, and since we have explored some of the sexist madness in our discussion on primary and affective sexuality, our main concern will be genital madness.

Two kinds of genital madness exist: normal and abnormal. Normal genital behavior is mad when it violates, impedes, or does not promote healthy growth, but still falls within the cultural confines of sanctioned norms. Thus, normal sex offenders are not punished or hospitalized, but are accepted as normal partly because their madness does not directly upset others' lives. In fact, we often condone and encourage normal madness, as we shall see. On the other hand, abnormal sex offenders are usually punished and sometimes hospitalized. Their actions, such as child molestation and rape, deviate from and directly upset the lives of normal people. Although abnormal and normal modes of madness are both similar to and differ from each other, a key point is to consider genital madness not only as abnormal—behavior that "they" can do—but also as normal—behavior that "we" can do. Let us consider some of the more common and pernicious modes of mad sexuality.

NORMAL SEXUAL MADNESS

Genitalism

Genitalism means that our ultimate concern is genital gratification so that life and especially people are ultimately seen in terms of genitality without authentic caring. We become sexual people whose main guiding force is genital sex. Although we may deny that we live according to a sex principle that posits physical genitality as our primary value, experientially our lives betray us. Experiencing others ultimately as objects to be used for sexual satisfaction, we see and make others (and ourselves) less than we are. Our world, the ways in which we experience reality, becomes genitalized so that almost everybody and every situation present possibilities for genital satisfaction.

Although we may be sophisticated enough to show concern for others, our behavior is essentially in service of self-satisfaction. So when we do not get what we want from one person, we withdraw and look for somebody else. We live according to a playboy philosophy: we are not mature persons, but boys who play. Being immersed in genitality without caring, we may appear vital and carefree but we fail to grow in love. Consequently, we may be normally adjusted but still mad.

Actually, some sexually frustrated people may admire or envy our playboy or playgirl life. It may seem that we are really enjoying life and constantly having new experiences, and persons who emphasize minimal satisfaction or who repress sexuality may be ambivalently attracted by our sexual dynamism. We may be good-looking, suave, and have the techniques to get what we want. And though we may have a high potential for violence, we are seldom intrusive and disruptive. Consequently, we are mad persons who are at least accepted as normal.

The ease and availability of sex encourage and facilitate genital sexualism. It is easier now than in the past for us to find partners and to move in public without embarrassment. Social establishments like bars, clubs, and apartments may cater to those seeking sex. Prostitution and pornography can also stimulate and feed our hunger, supply our demands, and help to maintain and promote our madness. The prostitute, for example, diagnoses and treats the sexually mad person, and the fee varies according to the expertise and the kind and length of treatment. Pornography nurtures genitalism by taking sex out of healthy context. The easy excitement and immediate gratification of prostitution and pornography, however, leads to numbing emptiness, fragmentation, and superficiality.

Consider a clever playboy. He learns how to play the game of "making" a woman. He may learn that some women can be seduced by dependent honesty, sincere loneliness, and desperate frustration, and he plays these roles for women who satisfy his needs. Or he may become an expert in sensing the loneliness of women who will do anything for some comfort and affirmation. After displaying some honest concern, he "offers" himself to her. Or playing a strong and suave role, he tries to overpower women, especially those who expect to be overpowered.

Women can also play sexual games just as well as, or better than, men. A woman can learn how to manipulate a man, how to play on his guilt and responsibility, and how to make him think he is seducing her. A woman, for example, may learn to present herself in an erotic but controlled way, and when a man responds, she can accept, reject, tolerate, manipulate, or exploit him; in any case she plays him for what he is—a fool. Or while playing the lonely, dependent, and desperate role, she may bilk a man for what he is worth, or she may play the part of a comforting and understanding person who mothers and castrates. She may simply move in on a man and overpower him.

We can play heterosexual games. We can make an implicit contract to satisfy each other, and though our mutual agreement is seldom overt, it is real. The contract is made on the basis of self-satisfaction, not on giving. We covertly communicate to each other: If you satisfy me, then I'll satisfy you. If one person breaks the contract, that is, one does not satisfy the other or asks for more than the contract calls for, then the second party withdraws.

Whatever game is played, no permanent commitment is made. In fact, sometimes the only commitment is not to be committed. The script sounds like this: "We can have a relationship, but with no strings attached. We can enjoy each other, but sooner or later we will part. There should be no hard feelings or attachments. We should not expect anything more." Life, however, does not usually follow such a script. Women (and men, more subtly) often feel empty, frustrated, and lonely when such a relationship ends. It seems that though these women understood the contract, their intimate giving called for a permanent commitment—a preverbal promise that was not fulfilled. Men, however, can often put their feelings aside more easily than women, or perhaps they do not involve themselves as fully as women do. Of course, women can act similarly to men and men similarly to women. Whatever the situation, such sexual madness stresses the physical and functional dimensions but minimizes, hides, or represses the spiritual. Consequently, the relationship is temporary and fails to promote growth.

Like any mad form of sexual activity, genitalism makes sense. We have seen that genital activity can satisfy basic needs, take away tensions, and help us feel at ease. Especially if we feel basically at odds with ourselves and others, repress sexuality, or live relatively disembodied lives, we can feel a certain completeness and tranquility along with quasi-fun. If life is complicated and tense because of overwork or environmental stress, genital sex offers a pleasant relief. If we live rational, functional, or spiritual lives, genitalism can offer us the illusion of being embodied and grounded. Some of us may only feel a sense of solidarity and security in sexuality so that life without genital sex would be unreal and boring. A celibate life would make no sense to us at all.

Genital behavior also becomes mad when its key force is the functional. For instance, as sexual technocrats we may be proficient in every sexual technique but fail to encounter a person. We may seem "to perform" well but may actually be hiding behind the most sophisticated techniques. Spontaneity, play, discovery, and surrender can easily be repressed and replaced by cognition, work, planning, and control. Such functional sex is doomed to be short-lived because the spirit of sex is lost.

The power experienced in sexuality can also be mad. For instance, a normal madman can feel power is his ability "to make" and penetrate a woman. A normal madwoman can feel powerful in making the male helpless in her arms while quietly smiling at his impotence. When we use sex only for self-gratification, we exploit others and degrade ourselves.

Our mad desire for power in sex is often a compensation for inferiority toward our own and the other sex. Perhaps more men than women use their power and sexuality as a means of compensating for their inadequate identity and fear of sex. As long as they have women underneath them, men can feel a false sense of superiority. Men can fool themselves into feeling that their genital encounters make up for a tenuous sense of primary identity. Genital sex itself is never a valid answer to questions of self-identity.

Genital sex can be madly important to normality in another way. It can be one of the few areas where some of us may have moments beyond normality. Since genital sexuality can transcend normal time and space, sex can be experienced as a timeless affair—at least for the moment. A genital encounter can also transcend normal dichotomies such as pleasure and pain, mind and body. We can in a sense come close to death and at the same time feel most ourselves, simultaneously experiencing pleasurable pain and a painful pleasure. Thus, genital sex can offer us unique advantages: it maintains normality and gives us moments of relative abnormality. Especially if our spiritual life is not furthered or embodied, sex can be a mad replacement for spirituality.

Such normal sexuality is mad because it is without care, commitment, and responsibility. Rather than promoting life, it merely maintains and can destroy it. Genitality is not integrated within the whole person and often is a displacement of wholeness and spirituality. Our irresponsible and selfish stand toward genitality prevents us from hearing the deeper call of genital sex—committed love. Since sex without love gives only temporary satisfaction, not growth in permanent fulfillment, genitalism ultimately leads to frustration and emptiness.

It is important to realize that genitalism is often an implicit move toward spirituality. When we are promiscuous in genital relations, we are often seeking lasting fulfillment deep within ourselves. We feel a subtle and repressed existential guilt that points to our lack of wholeness—a guilt that indicts our integrity, questions our dignity, and states that we are capable of being more. Although we might act "cool"—be physically and functionally settled and competent, we silently cry for wholeness. The sense of striving toward a whole and spiritual life is often discovered in the apparent nonsense of genitalism.

In time, genitalism wears thin. We find we have less energy, attraction, and desire, and we hear the call of other realities. Sex is no longer as vital and exciting as it once was, and it fails to answer deeper questions. Sex fails to meet the summons of impending death—to live fully and wholly. In facing death, we find that we are dissociated and displaced—cut off from our spirit. Our sexual search for meaning eventually leaves us lifeless. In our sexual madness, nevertheless, we can listen to the search for permanent meaning.

Driving Others Sexually Mad

We have indicated how we can defend ourselves against sexuality because we have learned that sexuality is bad, evokes punishment or unpleasant feelings, or is simply something not to consider. We may learn to assume that an essential experience is unessential, a good experience is bad, and a sacred experience only profane. We can learn to dislike experiences we really like. For instance, sexuality comes naturally and pleasantly to children, but because of disapproval, they can learn to dislike sexuality. We have also indicated that we can learn to be what we are really not, that is, nonsexual beings. We can expend much time and energy pretending to be asexual when in fact we are sexual. And some of us can pretend to be who we really are—we can repress sexuality and then pretend to be sexual.

In this section, we will use a framework of Searles to consider some normal modes of intersexual madness.[1] Most of these sexual games are normally mad ways which can evoke abnormal madness. The main dynamic of such interpersonal madness is that certain transactions activate areas in a person which are simultaneously in opposition to each other. Thus, a person must be and must not be at the same time.

One way of driving another sexually mad is to point out sexual experiences that a person is unaware of and that are inconsistent with his/her self-image. For example, part of a man's self-image may be to have no sexual feelings or fantasies perhaps because he was taught that sexuality is evil. He may convincingly and sincerely argue with a woman that he has no sexual feelings even though the woman stimulates him by her dress, demeanor, or simply by being a woman. As he denies sexual stimulation, the woman forcefully shows him physical evidence of his sexual feelings. The man is then caught in a bind: he must value being sexless and yet he has clearly been shown evidence that he is sexual. Thus, he may feel very threatened and perhaps helpless to deal with his new awareness.

A relatively common way of driving another person sexually mad is to stimulate a person sexually in settings where gratification would be disastrous. For example, at social gatherings a man may be sexually suggestive, seductive, and stimulating to a woman, but when they are alone, the man is insulted if the woman becomes sexually assertive.

---

1. Robert Searles, "The Effort to Drive the Other Person Crazy—An Element in the Etiology and Psychotherapy of Schizophrenia," *British Journal of Medical Psychology*, 32:1, 1959.

Or he can be intimidated and withdraw, or he might plead innocence at her suggestions. In a social situation, he feels safe enough to play sexual games, but alone with a woman, he becomes impotent.

A similar game is the rapid alternation of stimulation and frustration. Consider a woman who speaks of sexuality in a suggestive and sensuous way. She seems to encourage such talk and be open to explore sexuality not only verbally but also behaviorally. When the man begins to encourage such speech and moves physically closer, she changes the subject or becomes mildly insulted by his sexual advances. But when the man withdraws or cools off, she begins to stimulate him again. This on-and-off approach can drive a man or a woman sexually mad.

Another mode of intersexual madness is to relate to a person simultaneously on two unrelated levels. For instance, a female teacher may be speaking about theoretical physics and at the same time be intentionally or unintentionally sexually seductive in dress and manner. This mode of behavior can pull the student in two opposite directions: the functionally theoretical and the sexually concrete. If the student were to focus on the sexual, the teacher could deny its existence and reprimand the student as a lascivious and immature person. Or this sexual game could be a safe way of making a choice: to have or not have sex with the student. When the student is sexually stimulated, the teacher has the choice and time to explore the possibility with him while never admitting any responsibility for the situation. Confusing? Yes, and mad.

While discussing sexuality, a teacher, for example, might switch erratically from one emotional wave length to another. He might speak theoretically and coldly to his female students about the purity and transcendence of sexuality until they are thoroughly bored or perhaps interested. He then switches to earthy and warm language. If some of the students become excited by this approach, he again switches to a very abstract and cold demeanor. These alternations can put students in a bind and confuse them.

Switching topics while maintaining the same sexual wave length can have the same effect. For example, a man may speak erotically about sexuality to a woman, and when she becomes excited, he changes the subject to asexual spirituality while maintaining his eroticism. On the cognitive level he denies sexuality while speaking about spirituality, but his behavior promotes sexuality. The woman may then become confused, frustrated, or perhaps angry. Or, he might share his insight on life in an erotic way, and then if he sees her becoming excited, he talks about friendship or morality while maintaining his eroticism. In this way the man gets vicarious sexual satisfaction and maintains his holy image. If she should confront his eroticism, he could deny its existence, make her feel guilty, or safely choose to implement or deny his sexual feelings. In any case, he is not being honest with her and often times dishonest with himself.

It might be mentioned that these mad sexual transactions are not the same as flirting. Flirting can be a way to open up possibilities for deeper relationships. Instead of promoting madness, flirting gives us the freedom to move in or out of a situation. Flirting can be a way of inviting a person to come closer, a way of testing limits, a friendly and pleasant way of practicing affective sexuality. Mad sexual relationships, however, are not in service of respectful transactions, and they impede our ability to discern the true meaning of experience.

Masturbation

In the recent past, masturbation was often considered one of the worst sins. When people masturbated, they neither passed go nor collected two hundred dollars, but went straight to hell and often died of guilt on the way. Many contemporary approaches go almost to the opposite extreme by considering masturbation as a sensible source of pleasure, a convenient tension reducer, or a way to realize body potential. Many mental health specialists say that it is a healthy practice.

Yet, not many authorities—parents and teachers— would actively or publicly encourage others to masturbate. Although a teacher may feel that masturbation is healthy, he or she would not suggest that students masturbate. Our position is that most masturbation is neither healthy nor unhealthy, but is normal. Masturbation is normal because most people do it from time to time and because it satisfies basic needs and reduces tensions.

Masturbation is seldom unhealthy in and of itself, but it can be an unhealthy symptom of a more basic problem. For example, a person who lives in a fantasy world and never risks intimacy in reality may be a compulsive masturbator. Such a compulsion is unhealthy because it is likely to be based on a schizoid existence. Such unhealthy masturbation, however, is relatively infrequent.

Although masturbation is usually not unhealthy, nevertheless it is not healthy. Since masturbation can maintain us, reduce tension, and evoke pleasure, it is usually normal. But masturbation can be more or less mad because it does not promote and can impede integral growth—especially spiritual growth.

Of course, there are many kinds of masturbatory activities. Adolescents who are coming into genitality in a new way usually masturbate for reasons different from those of adults. Early adolescents usually feel the urgency and confusion of genitality and experience pressure from their peers. But the attitudes formed in adolescence can have a great impact on the adult years. Adolescents who feel that masturbation is a healthy practice may carry this attitude throughout life, and those who experience unhealthy guilt will probably feel the same way when they become adults. Our main concern is adult masturbation.

One of the seductive features of masturbation is that it is an easy and accessible way to reduce tension and to explore genitality. Masturbation usually supports a fantasy where we can explore any kind of sexual activity. Although fantasy can be in service of reality, fantasy is unreal in that there are no limits such as weight, smell, risk, responsibility. Masturbation lends itself to fantasy where we do not have to experience anxieties such as being frightened, rejected, or impotent, but can have the illusion of being the perfect lover. In fantasy, there are no limits and the other always says yes. Masturbatory fantasy is genital pleasure without risk and responsibility.

There are many reasons, besides accessibility and pleasure, for masturbating. Masturbation can help us to know our bodies and can give vitality to life. This is not to say, however, that this is the only or best way to learn about and to vitalize our body. In fact, since masturbation reaffirms and reinforces embodiment, it can be especially tempting to a person who leads a disembodied life. For example, persons who lead very intellectual lives may be more tempted to masturbate than average people. Or persons who dedicate their lives to spirituality may paradoxically be more tempted to masturbate. Especially in our western culture, spirituality tends to be a disembodied process, and therefore masturbation can be an attempt to embody oneself. The affirmation and pleasure of such embodiment can be self-reinforcing so that masturbation can become a habit that is difficult to stop.

Masturbation can also be a yearning for intimacy and completeness. In fantasy, we may safely seek to express what we need or want in reality, or we may try to complete our personhood. Masturbation can often be an attempt at intimacy, which usually means that we are not sufficiently intimate or whole in day-to-day living. For example, persons who live highly rational and functional lives may not embody themselves sufficiently in everyday activities and therefore may be more inclined to masturbate. Masturbation may satisfy the yearning for completeness and intimacy, but not in a growth-oriented way. Masturbation is actually a form of self-intimacy that can impede intimacy with another. The paradox is that the yearning for interpersonal intimacy in masturbation can be impeded by such masturbatory self-intimacy.

One of the most subtle forms of nonsense in masturbation is that an adult's initial decision to masturbate does not emerge from genital needs, but emerges out of nongenital experiences. That is, our initial option to masturbate often springs from nongenital experiences. Masturbation can be an attempt to fulfill loneliness and to escape feelings of anxiety and depression. When we masturbate, we can shut off the world of pain, alienation, and imperfection, and feel some semblance of being one with ourselves. We can escape from and fail to listen to and learn from our painful feelings of self-discovery, and consequently we are less able to surrender to others.

Most people who masturbate have a desire to be intimate with others. Though fantasies support this intimacy, masturbatory fantasies can run contrary to real love wherein we have moments of completion but are never absolutely complete or without imperfection and risk. In fact, there can be an inverse ratio between real intimacy and such masturbatory activities. Although we want to love, we are often scared to risk being hurt, imperfect, or lonely. Instead, we may choose the immediate gratification, illusory perfection, and temporary fulfillment of masturbation, and invest our love narcissistically in self. The more we are interpersonally intimate in reality, the less need we have to masturbate.

Different persons may masturbate for different reasons. Persons who masturbate several times every six months may relieve tension and compensate for a lack of emotional expression, but they are still escaping from themselves. Such persons should try to listen to and learn from their tension. Obviously, these persons differ from celibates or noncelibates who masturbate daily as an escape into fantasy because they are deathly afraid of reality.

Persons who feel guilty about masturbating should listen to what their guilt says and to what kind of guilt it is. Ideally, we should not feel guilty simply because we broke a rule or commandment, but we should feel guilty about what that rule or commandment points to. A superego guilt, in fact, can push us toward masturbation even more strongly. We feel guilty when we masturbate, which builds tension, which forces us to masturbate. Guilt could also emerge from making fantasy an overcompensation or a replacement for reality. An authentic guilt could indicate running from painful self-awareness or a lack of the creative control and discipline needed to accept and listen to the pain of self-discovery. Healthy guilt indicates that we are not living as well as we realistically can. Instead of feeling superego guilt for masturbating, we should feel guilty because we are being less than we can be. Rather than being centered around doing something wrong, such guilt evokes the absence of what is right or best. Thus, our approach focuses more on the good that is missing, than on the bad.

In light of our view of primary sexuality, there may be some differences between male and female masturbation. Aside from cultural programming that promotes double standards between the sexes, men usually find it easier to separate their masturbatory activities from their other activities. Men can masturbate quickly, put their masturbatory activities aside, and then engage in other activities. To be sure, women may also be capable of this kind of approach but usually are not. Women, on the other hand, are more likely to carry masturbatory effects along with them, and such effects are more likely to have an influence on the other areas of their lives. Also, since women usually take longer to come to orgasm, not only physically but also psychologically, they usually need and take more time during masturbation. Furthermore, orgasm can be more complex and its consequences can linger longer in women than in men. Although masturbation does not necessarily kill spiritual meaning, the peripheral self-reinforcement, the tendency to foster fantasy, and the narcissistic escape from deeper self-awareness impede self-discovery, self-actualization, and self-surrender. Masturbation is often a normal way of escaping the pain of self-acceptance and discovery.

Genital Dysfunctions

Much meaning can be embedded in the genital dysfunctions of "frigidity" and "impotence," particularly in indicating basic attitudes toward self and other. First of all, "frigidity" and "impotence" are terms imbued with sexist meaning. For instance, frigidity denotes negativity—coldness and rigidity—and connotes a lack of warmth and flexibility along with docility, dependence, and unconditional receptivity. Being frigid can mean that a woman is not living up to sexist standards. Likewise, impotence denotes a lack of power and connotes a failure to perform, to take an aggressive stand, or "to be on top." In fact being receptive, nurturing, or affectionate can be interpreted as symptoms of impotence rather than of health. With this sexism in mind, let us reflect on the madness of frigidity and impotence.

Consider frigidity as a no to sexual surrender and move away from another. Such genital dysfunction can be a form of self-rejection. If a woman feels unworthy or does not feel sexually significant, frigidity can be an affirmation of her basic attitude. And if a woman feels rejected and depressed, frigidity is also understandable.

Some women may remain celibate or "choose" celibacy because of a fear of intimacy with men. Some simply withdraw from most forms of heterosexual contact, and others overcompensate by becoming hostile toward men—the enemy. In such cases, celibacy is motivated by frigidity—not just genital frigidity but a more basic primary and affective frigidity. Instead of making sense of such feelings as hurt, resentment, and fear (which probably make positive sense), these women withdraw and sometimes fight. Frigidity is the price they pay for being less than they really can be.

Frigidity, however, may be a sign of a struggle for health. For instance, if a marriage has slowly dissipated instead of growing in health, frigidity can make positive sense. To surrender authentically can be almost impossible or a pathetic pretense. Or if a woman realizes clearly for the first time that she has been manipulated and patronized, her frigidity may be a loud no to this kind of treatment. Ideally, a woman ought to listen to her frigidity and learn to cope more directly.

In a similar way, impotence can have positive and negative meanings. If a man feels leveled, lacks enthusiasm, and feels basically depressed, impotence is an understandable consequence. Or if a man has always focused on the physical side of genitality as contrasted with affection and love, impotence can easily emerge, especially during middle age. Such a man is no longer as physically energetic as in the past, and moreover there are spiritual demands that the physical cannot meet. Thus, if a man has dissociated genitality from spirituality, impotence can easily occur.

Perhaps more with a man than a woman, fear of "poor physical performance" can pressure a man into impotence. Rather than performing poorly, he does not engage in sex at all or he has infrequent and quick sex. Though most men do not ordinarily lose the physiological ability to maintain an erection, quick and crass relations can be a form of impotence. A common factor is loss of psychological interest and spiritual enthusiasm for sexuality. Impotence may be a way of escaping from the demands of love—from being wholly present.

Genital impotence often is a symptom of existential impotence—of feeling inadequate with women. An impotent man often feels intimidated not only genitally but also affectively and existentially so that he withdraws or fails to take a solid stand. Some impotent men may unconsciously choose to be celibate partly because of their basic impotence. Others get married and practice physical and fast sex to overcompensate for their spiritual inadequacy. As these men grow older, they find it more difficult to hide their primary sexual impotence, and consequently withdraw from most forms of intimacy. They may focus on the functional aspects of living and withdraw from the spiritual, or their spiritual lives may become weak and progressively lifeless.

Homogenitalism

Homosexuality is a controversial and unsettling topic. Culturally, many persons think that homosexuality is a perversion, a disease, evil, or at least not good. And others hold that homosexuals can function just as well as heterosexuals and that it is only a matter of choosing an alternate sex life. Others harbor ambivalent and ambiguous feelings about homosexuality, and almost everyone is becoming increasingly aware of its complexity through literature, the mass media, and private discussion.

Along with these cultural changes, research projects such as the Kinsey Report, which stated that 37 percent of the total male population has had at least one physical homosexual experience between adolescence and old age, tend to challenge or change consciousness. Furthermore, the issue has been debated on television and radio, and homosexuals have "come out" individually and in groups. Thus, the homosexual question is more explicit and unsettling now that in the recent past, and the result is more openness and willingness to discuss and understand homosexuality.

In light of these and other changes, the professional stand on homosexuality has also changed. On December 15, 1973, the American Psychiatric Association's thirteen-member board of trustees voted unanimously to remove homosexuality from the category of mental illness. The official psychiatric view is that homosexuality in itself is no longer professionally considered a sexual deviation, but individuals can be diagnosed as having a "sexual orientation disturbance" when they are bothered by, in conflict with, or wish to change their sexual orientations; otherwise, one can presume that homosexuality is normal. But this decision by the APA board of trustees was challenged by many psychiatrists throughout the United States so that at present homosexuality is still heatedly debated. Some think that homosexuals can be as healthy as heterosexuals; others contend that people should have a choice in their sexual life; and still others hold that homosexuality is an indication of maladjusted development. Our thesis is that genital relations between members of the same sex is not healthy, but that love of the same sex is healthy and necessary.

Distinctions and Definitions. Strictly speaking, homosexuality means homogenitality. Those who choose a homosexual life-style indicate that sexually they prefer and desire genital relations with a member of the same sex. With the latter homosexuals feel comfortable and affirmed, while with the opposite sex they feel uncomfortable, impotent, resentful, scared, or simply indifferent when genital relations are possible. When people consistently, and over a long period of time, yearn to be genitally intimate and behave genitally with the same sex, they are true homosexuals. To have or have had some sexual desires for or fantasies about the same sex or to have engaged in sexuality with the same sex does not necessarily mean, however, that a person is a homosexual. The life-styles of homosexuals are permeated with and motivated by genital relations with the same sex, rather than being periodic. Especially when lonely, empty, or depressed, homosexuals turn to a sexual relationship with a member of the same sex as their saving grace.

Furthermore, physical attractiveness and genital gratification are often very important—and, rather than leading to genitality, homosexual relationships often begin with genital relations. Although there may be a yearning to be more than physically intimate, the accent tends to be on the physical so that the spiritual dimension is forgotten, minimized, or dissociated. A key and frequent dynamic of homosexuality is that homosexuals try to find or affirm themselves in the same sex as a means of gaining and keeping their sexual identity.

There are no conclusive theories about the causes of homosexuality. Some theories and evidence propose organic factors as causes, but such physical approaches have recently lost credibility. There is no indication of hormonal imbalance in the homosexual nor is there any hard evidence of inheritance of such leanings. Some researchers, however, think that during a critical period in childhood a preferred sexual object or person can become firmly entrenched in the brain.

More accepted approaches to homosexuality are that it is a learned preference or based on certain psychosocial conditions in a person's development. Research indicates that a so-called typical male homosexual had a very close relationship with a mother who was strong, intimate, and dominating, while the father was rejecting, cold, or distant. Thus, according to this theory, most male homosexuals have an overprotective and close-binding mother along with a detached, absent, or brutal father. Such an approach indicates that a homosexual needs no other relationship with a woman because he has his mother, and suggests reasons why a homosexual might have ambivalent feelings about entering an intimate heterosexual relationship. As one homosexual put it, "I really don't need or want a relationship with a woman because I have my mother." This theory also suggests that a homosexual futilely seeks his absent father in other males. In other words, if a boy has a warm affectionate relationship with his father, homosexuality is unlikely to occur.

There can be many reasons for a father's absence. If a man is separated or divorced, he may not see his son or other children very often or not at all. Perhaps because of death, the father is no longer physically present or painfully present in his absence. A father may be absent because of too much work and traveling or because of going to war. Though the father may not really have much choice about being absent, the son will nevertheless miss his father. More frequently, however, the father is physically present but psychologically and spiritually absent. Such a "phantom father" hides behind his newspaper or keeps out of the way and never really touches or plays with his children. A father who has a sensitive and poetic son may withdraw from and reject him because he is not athletic. Whatever the case, the son feels he is rejected or at least not affirmed by a man. This does not mean that all boys who lack a physical or psychological father will emerge as homosexuals. Their sexual identity, however, is likely to be impaired unless a surrogate father is introduced into the family situation.

If the father or a man is absent, the mother will be under pressure to assume the role of the man and take over more family responsibility. Thus, a woman who does not have the support of a husband may be more inclined to be dominant, overprotective, and binding. If the mother is to be blamed, she should also be given credit for taking the responsibility. Actually, the father is probably more at fault than the mother in such a situation. But since the father recedes into the background or withdraws from the situation, he is less likely to be noticed.

The psychological research on homosexual females, which is relatively sparse, indicates that homosexual females come from families in which there are cruel fathers and martyred mothers. Oftentimes homosexual females are highly developed in dominance, status seeking, intellectual efficiency, and endurance. The theory proposes that they may have developed such characteristics to compensate for the possibility of males once more causing chaos in their lives as they did when they were children. One recurrent differentiation between male and female homosexuals is that the female has longer periods of attachment to one partner. While male relationships are usually short-lived and throughout the life span include many partners, lesbian relationships last much longer and are more likely to be far fewer in number.

The main nonsense of homosexuality as we see it is that homogenitality lacks and excludes permanent commitment. In homogenitality, the parts do not fit physically, psychologically, or spiritually. Homogenitality, unlike heterogenitality, neither incorporates more than the two persons nor points to a transcendent commitment. Thus, what many homosexuals are really seeking—to feel permanently at home and to grow in love—is not possible in homogenital relations. The primary thesis is that "homogenitality"—genital relations between members of the same sex—is not healthy, but love of the same sex is healthy and necessary.

Some opponents might say that homosexual marriages or permanent relationships do exist, but those that last for substantial periods of time are rare. In fact, little if any sociological data exists to support such long-term relationships. As for those homosexuals who do live together for a long time, genital relations are usually absent or minimal. Such partners go outside their relationship to satisfy their genital needs so that their ongoing commitment is more of a celibate friendship. In short, homogenital relationships run contrary to the process of authentic genitality; that is, homogenitality does not promote progressive and lasting fulfillment as is possible with heterogenital relationships. To be sure, all heterogenital relationships do not promote integral and ongoing growth; nevertheless, such permanent growth is possible in heterogenitality. It must be emphasized, however, that homosexuals can live authentically in many ways, but that their homogenital love is temporary, not permanent.

When we put persons into a homosexual category, though we may know better, we still tend to treat them all alike. The ever-present and simplistic danger of identifying a person with a part of his makeup, in this case sexuality, can be an unjust judgement. Homosexuals probably differ as much as heterosexuals. Some are unhealthy and need help, and others are normal in that they can cope with reality, succeed, and look and act like anyone else. It is their sexual preference that is abnormal. Homosexuals are normal if they are free from psychopathology and have a high degree of adjustment, and, more important, if they can live a life of love with men and women. Functionally and socially male homosexuals may get along with women as well as or better than heterosexuals. Some question, however, whether female homosexuals get along quite well with men. The main problem of homosexuality is that homogenital relationships do not promote love and can impede and violate love. Thus, though homosexuals may live lives of love, homogenitality is not recommended and is considered a serious impediment to love.

Some persons have homosexual tendencies or cravings which they manage to control. Although their orientation is primarily homosexual in that they crave intimacy and genital relations with the same sex, they nevertheless respect and function well with both sexes. Though they have homosexual feelings and fantasies, they seldom if ever engage in homogenital relations. These homosexuals are celibate.

In fact, some homosexuals may enter a religious community and live a vowed life, including celibacy.

Sometimes, however, such persons can be unjustly prevented from entering personal and professional areas because of their homosexual tendencies. Homosexuals should be judged on the basis of their whole life, not simply on their sexual preference. Each person should be accepted because he has the call, the aptitude, motivation, and personality for a profession and a life form such as the religious life. Certainly if a candidate cannot live the religious life, which includes being chaste and celibate, then this person should not be accepted. The same can be said for heterosexual persons. Straights and often gays need to be aware that homosexuals are less different from and more similar to heterosexuals.

A frequent experience of many is transitory homosexuality. For example, persons who have homogenital experiences perhaps once or several times in their lives are usually not homosexual. Despite these experiences, their life-style is not basically homosexual. Transitory homosexuality can happen to persons who are sensitive but have learned to repress or to overcontrol feelings. For example, a vowed religious who comes from a good but puritanical family which neglected affective expression can become involved with another religious who promotes affective expression. Both persons may become so emotionally involved that they fall into genitality as a mode of full expression. These religious should not identify themselves as homosexuals, though they should strive to understand the sense and nonsense of their behavior. And their superior should not call them impure, evil, lustful, or play on their guilt; this rank-pulling behavior is unjust and may serve the superior's madness. Ideally, these people should get help from a competent person who understands and appreciates the religious life.

Or consider two women who are deep friends. These women love each other and may come to express themselves deeply and openly. Especially in the initial phases of their friendship, they may want to give all and in every way, including genitally, but usually after awhile they realize that their genital encounters will eventually destroy their friendship. Consequently, they set limits and abstain from genital love. These women are not actually lesbians, but two persons who originally repressed and minimized themselves, especially affectively. Their homosexual experiences should not be condoned, but neither should their experiences condemn them to a life of guilt and withdrawal.

How to relate sexually as man to man or woman to woman is often a subtle and crucial problem that is probably more common with men. Most forms of culture in this country make it very difficult for a man to be intimate with another man. To do more than shake hands may be seen almost as a perversion in some subcultures. Furthermore, many men, both celibate and noncelibate, have a weak sexual identity that they often misinterpret as latent homosexuality. Consequently, any expression of love toward a man can easily evoke unnecessary guilt and anxiety or at least a manifestation of homophobia. Women, both personally and culturally, are often more comfortable in this homosocial realm. Culturally, for example, two women hugging is all right, but two men embracing often evoke judgments that range from tolerance to arrest.

Part of the problem may be due to decades of forbidding and punishing friendship and the expression of feelings. Many people do not know how to form healthy friendships and often feel guilty for wanting them. A possible consequence is that overrestriction and repression of affect can build up emotional pressures that eventually lead to over-involvement and perhaps unchaste experiences. One extreme can engender the opposite extreme.

A subtle force is the relatively recent approach that fosters "intimacy," friendships, sharing, and emotional expression. For instance, people (old as well as young) are encouraged to foster intimate friendship or a relationship with "deeply personal feelings" while forgetting about or minimizing the complexity of sexuality, the strength of historical programming, and the true nature of celibacy. Good and naive people can be led to believe that any act is good if sincerely and honestly performed in the name of "love." In heterosexual relationships as well, modern man is especially adept at giving such a "loving love" that is in service of his narcissism. Such people can end up feeling guilty and inadequate, be seriously wounded and crushed, or forget authentic celibate relations and consequently lose their spirit.

Intimacy, affection, and love can take many forms which can be congruent or incongruent with one another. For instance, intimacy can be an expression and affirmation of healthy love, or it can be an exercise in mutual masturbation, narcissistic manipulation, or self-effacing dependency. Actually, most acts of love are neither directly intimate nor deeply affectionate.

Affection when given for the good of the other is good, but when given for self, it can be destructive. People can be killed with so-called care. To pressure people to share feelings, to induce guilt for not emoting, to "pray" for the emotionally restricted, or to reflect others' feelings without their permission are pseudotherapeutic and often violent.

When people feel compelled to be intimate and affectionate, chaos along with injured hearts can result. To assume that intimacy and affection are always good and to be fostered leads to guilt, alienation, or sticky and exclusive relationships. To be sure, healthy friendship can and should in some way be affectionate and intimate. A gentle look, an assuring touch, a warm glance, a compassionate word, a playful smile, a good nudge, and a respectful embrace can be expressions of affective sexuality and our love for each other.

Problems emerge when homosocial (or heterosocial) friends desire to behave genitally. In such a situation, friends should not and do not have to encourage feelings and behavior that foster genital experiences. Pseudonotions of intimacy and affection can easily activate genital desires and pressure friends to engage each other genitally. Particularly when spiritual values and experiences are forgotten or repressed, one-sided erotic desires can take over and strongly demand genital gratification. Still, not all eroticism is evoked by spiritual fragmentation and/or by selfish and possibly well-intentioned motives. Genital feelings can naturally arise with an integral and loving stance. Then the challenge is to accept the genital feelings and suppress, mortify, sublimate, or integrate them.

Another problem arises when homosociality, how a person relates to the same sex socially and affectively, is confused with homosexuality. Such a relationship can be a subtle and crucial problem usually more to men than to women partly because our culture makes it difficult for men to be appropriately close with one another. To do more than shake hands in some subcultures is almost seen as a perversion or certainly not tolerated. Furthermore, since many men have a precarious sexual identity that they might misinterpret as latent homosexuality and since they are programmed to feel that affection leads to genitality, any expression of affection toward a man can evoke unnecessary guilt and anxiety or a manifestation of homophobia. Or going to the opposite extreme, some men become very chummy and adolescent as an indirect way of expressing their repressed affectivity. Frequent adolescent expressions of affection and semi-erotic kidding may not be a sign of latent homosexuality but indicative of immature sexuality.

Another possibility is "heterophobia," fear of heterosexual involvement. By focusing on the same sex, some people can escape their fear of the other sex. For example, a man may focus exclusively on men as a way of escaping his fear of women. When confronted with women, he becomes withdrawn, condescending, or just plain scared. Whatever the situation, this man cannot feel comfortable and open with women. Or think of a woman who craves intimacy with another woman because she never learned to deal with men. Perhaps her past experiences were traumatic in that she was abused or rejected by men so that her quasi and transitory homosexual leanings may be a cover for unresolved heterosexual experiences or for immature sexuality.

Another subtle possibility is repressed sexuality that seeks satisfaction with any person regardless of gender and age. Fixated and fragmented sexuality can move polymorphously—seeking many (or any) forms of gratification. Such people, for example, may find themselves being stimulated in the presence of the same sex or with adolescents. Such people are probably not homosexuals or youth molesters but people whose immature sexuality seeks (under certain conditions) some-body rather than no-body. By becoming more aware of and working through their heterosexual conflict and/or repressed and underdeveloped sexuality, people can transcend their quasi-homosexual propensities.

Our position is that we must be open to woman-woman and man-man sexual dialogue on the primary and affective planes. Homogenital behavior is neither healthy nor unhealthy (abnormally mad) but is normally mad. And feelings, fantasies, and actions that encourage or involve homogenital behavior should be listened to, understood, suppressed, sublimated, and integrated.

Masochism and Sadism

Although masochism and sadism can be abnormal when they are part of another offense such as rape, they are more often normal modes of madness. Let us briefly look at ourselves in terms of masochism and sadism.

Masochism means that our main and most important source of pleasure and meaning is pain. When we are sexually masochistic persons, we get our ultimate sexual pleasure and fulfillment from being hurt. Masochism does not refer to playful pain that can be part of healthy sexual relations, but to pain as an end in itself or as our ultimate concern. Pain, not love, is the redemptive experience.

We may want to hurt because of unconscious guilt and self-degradation. The punishment from self or others lessens guilt and can elicit unhealthy feelings of precarious worth. For example, a woman may feel angry and resentful toward men, but because of her conditioning to be docile, she may feel guilty and ask for or encourage sexual punishment. Instead of listening to her meaningful feelings, the punishment relieves her guilt and helps her to maintain her unhealthy source of worth—being servile to men. Or a man who represses sexual feelings and lives a numbed emotional life may ask to be constantly hurt in sex in order to stimulate some feelings of life, albeit painful. Such pain can punish him for the sin of sex and simultaneously let him feel sexual.

Sometimes it may be necessary to hurt another in service of truth, but such pain is neither an end in itself nor is it primarily intended as such. As sadists, we experience other sources of meaning as secondary to inflicting pain. We may not experience much contentment or pleasure other than in painful sex, and we may try to achieve power that compensates for weakness and resentment. For example, a man who harbors deep hurt and resentment toward women may make it his life task to hurt women in order to lower them and to give him a feeling of superiority. Or a woman's main source of superiority and pleasure may come from making a man beg for sex.

Pornography

Consider pornography as material or behavior whose primary purpose is to excite us genitally. To get a concrete understanding of the sense and nonsense of pornography, we will focus on pornographic books. What can be said of pornographic books, however, can also be said of other forms of pornography, especially of movies.

One reason that pornographic books are especially tempting is that they can satisfy our curiosity in easy and safe ways. Pornographic books and movies are more available than they were in the recent past so that we can easily gain access to them. Without anyone knowing, we can get an idea of what happens behind closed doors, and we can be stimulated without risk of real interpersonal involvement. As pornographic readers, we can also engage and test ourselves with the book's characters and/or pictures. And, unlike many other books, they are easy and pleasurable to read. Those of us who live too much from the neck up or who live disembodied lives can be especially vulnerable to pornography because it offers us a safe and easy way to embody ourselves, though not authentically. Especially if we are tense or highly involved in intellectual pursuits, pornography can offer an easy and pleasurable reading experience. As contrasted with intellectual reading, we need not analyze in depth or study the material but can let ourselves be pleasured. Pornography also may offer expedient and safe gratification to people who repress sexuality or who have inadequate sexual experiences. Sexual frustration can be safely lessened and gratification can be controlled.

Part of the nonsense is that pornography describes or shows sexual activities that happen mostly in our head and seldom in reality. The intent of pornography is to make the whole of life a genital orgy. Part of the nonsense is that sexuality is taken out of a true context and dissociated from our whole beings. It is very easy when reading pornographic books to see people only in sexual terms. Pornography also encourages us to take an unreal look at and to use ourselves and others for selfish satisfaction. Pornography can fool us into thinking that genitality can take the place of genuine caring.

Pornographic books can be especially negative when we read too many of them. Imagine yourself reading many pornographic books consecutively within a short period of time. During your pornographic binge, you may feel highly stimulated, less tense, and obtain needed relief. At the end, however, you will probably feel exhausted, empty, and shallow. This often happens because pornography only stimulates the surface of our personhood. Actually, pornography insults us by treating us as less than we really are.

Such experiences say that when we read pornography, we are not treating ourselves as well as we can. Reading pornography or seeing pornographic movies can mean that we sell ourselves short because we treat ourselves as sex objects. This does not mean that occasional pornography is unhealthy or will drive us crazy; pornography, however, is neither healthy nor good. Basically, the more mature and integrated we are, the less we need and want pornography.

Voyeurism and Exhibitionism

"Peeping" can be a normal or abnormal mad mode of sexuality, and sometimes it can be a function of curiosity. For example, sometimes adolescents accidently see parents undressed or making love, and they may be tempted to take a second look. When we live with others, we can stumble into a room where our mother or father (brother or sister) are undressed, or we may hear our parents making sexual love, and perhaps feel confused or guilty about wanting to hear more. Our guilt is unnecessary because our curiosity is natural and normal. Although parents are entitled to privacy and such curiosity should not be encouraged, nevertheless, sexual curiosity is a normal part of development.

Adolescents or adults may extend their curiosity by peeping at neighbors getting undressed. This kind of voyeurism can be primarily a matter of curiosity when the peeping is spontaneous and infrequent. But when we plan to peep and do so frequently, peeping becomes immature and probably unhealthy. Consider this Peeping Tom. "I don't know what gets into me. I can't help myself. At least twice a week, I go on these binges and try to watch someone get undressed. I know the schedule of some people so I can pretty well know when they are going to bed. If I can, I'll masturbate when I see some action. I know this is crazy. In fact, if I get caught, I could go to jail. I really need some help." This man is not simply curious, but he has an unhealthy compulsion to peep. His peeping is abnormally mad.

Such unhealthy peeping promotes sexual fantasy that replaces reality. A Peeping Tom can feel a strange sense of power in looking at another's private domain while not really being involved. The voyeur may engage the other in fantasy and often masturbates while fantasizing. Such looking and fantasizing present no interpersonal risk and responsibility, for when someone compulsively peeps, he uses others simply for his own satisfaction. Sexuality is made purely physical, and therefore unwhole. As with pornography, promotion of voyeurism reinforces the periphery of ourselves and militates against depth and integration.

An important point about a voyeur is that he can intrude on people's personal lives and get meaning from seeing people behave in ways that no one else sees. A Peeping Tom can use the private situation and pretend to make love in any way he desires without risk, rejection, commitment, or limits. Furthermore, he can get a special thrill when he sees "his woman" in public because he knows what she does and looks like in private. He may know her in ways that no one else knows her. His voyeurism gives him a taste of intimacy and power without risk and responsibility, feeds his fantasies, and usually supports masturbation.

More frequent than this private and abnormal voyeurism is social and normal peeping. We can dress and act in ways that invite more intimate glances, and fashion and mass communication can support our inclination to look at the more intimate parts of a person's body. Such normal peeping can make sense and nonsense. A woman, for example, may invite a man to look at her intimately by the way she dresses. If she shows herself sexually and suggestively, she may be asking for voyeurist attention. Ideally, instead of seeing only parts of her or viewing her as a sex object, the man could appreciate her whole being. He could let the part evoke the whole. Still, some persons' dress and demeanor can pressure us to dissociate or fragment them. Such public exhibitionism can promote "sexification"—making people sex objects.

Some of us may feel guilty when we see a normally covered part of the body uncovered or when we look at a physically attractive person. Immediately guilt feelings may be evoked and genitality stimulated. Generally this means that we have not integrated our sexuality. There is nothing wrong and there can be a lot right in admiring a person's embodiment. The crucial factor is to see the person as an embodied spirit, not as a despiritualized body.

Instead of taking a peek, a healthy approach would be to look more openly and intensely at whatever is shown. Instead of taking a side glance at a person, we can look straightforwardly in appreciation. We can see what is really there. If someone's dress and behavior invite more intimacy, especially genitality, we can freely choose what course of action to take and accept the consequences. We lose freedom when we do not see honestly and truthfully, and consequently we can more easily be seduced or withdraw in unnecessary guilt.

The abnormal exhibitionist is also a sexual madman who seldom gets close enough to touch. Such an exhibitionist constantly exposes his genitals for a number of reasons. He may want to shock a woman to get back at "women" for making him feel inferior, or he may look for some sort of affirmation that he is a man. In his unhealthy world, he somehow feels that showing his penis is a way of feeling superior. Actually, most exhibitionists always feel on center stage and believe they must perform for approving applause; however, they feel their performance is never quite adequate. When they feel inadequate, empty, and intimidated, and stress becomes overwhelming, they feel compelled to give the so-called grand performance—publicize their private parts.

We can be normal exhibitionists: we do not expose our genitals in public but expose ourselves too much in inappropriate situations. The woman who dresses suggestively to be affirmed and perhaps to confuse men may be an exhibitionist. Her main motivation is not aesthetic, but to manipulate men. Or a man who parades nude in his home or suggestively in public situations may be compensating for a lack of genuine sexual identity. Of course, some exhibitionism (showing oneself in the nude) can be an enjoyable part of and in service of genuine loving sex.

As exhibitionist and voyeurs, we can also complement one another in normal but mad ways. Pornography, for example, supplies voyeuristic demands. Men who want to peek at the intimate parts of women may be supplied by female exhibitionists. We would probably not dress and act sexually inappropriately unless others looked. Without demand, supply and service would soon decrease.

ABNORMAL SEXUAL MADNESS

Unlike normal sex offenders, abnormal sex offenders are usually considered to be criminals who are to be punished, incarcerated, and sometimes helped. We often judge them as the most detestable of persons, and we see ourselves as totally different from these abnormal people. Yet, we have seen that any sexual activity that uses and abuses ourselves and others is a sex offense regardless of its normality or abnormality. Some of us, however, may need abnormal sex offenders in order to criticize and displace our guilt on them, thereby giving ourselves the illusion of having healthy sex. This does not mean that normal and abnormal sex offenses are identical, but that both violate healthy sexuality.

The abnormal sex offender is seldom the dirty old man who lurks in the shadows waiting for the innocent virgin whom he rapes viciously. Most sex offenders (with the exception of most rapists) are usually not vicious and are often passive, sensitive, and intelligent. They are usually normal people except in this one realm. But abnormal sex offenders, unlike normal sex offenders, break the law and are socially disruptive.

Child Molestation

Consider a much detested sex offender: the child molester. Like most abnormal sex offenders, he probably feels anxiously small and inadequate with women, yet he wants to be close to them. In molesting a child, who is usually fondled and not raped, he feels the child is unlikely to reject him. He can be at ease with the child and feel some semblance of being a man to compensate for his precarious sexual identity. To be sure, the child molester is unhealthy and his actions are bad if for no other reasons than he exploits the child, represses experience, and satisfies himself in a mad way.

The victim, who is usually female, is often harmed less by the sex offender than by parents, authorities, and other concerned people. When we normal people reinforce unnecessary guilt or fear in a child, we can be almost as mad as the sex offender. Furthermore, since a relative or an acquaintance, not a stranger, is often the molester, the parents may feel threatened, confused, or embarrassed. Such an offense may evoke their own sexual ambivalence or madness. Whatever the case, we can overreact to protect ourselves.

For instance, a girl who has been molested may come from a family which represses sexuality and emotion. When a neighbor fondles her, she may feel sheepish and a bit guilty, but not overly frightened or guilty. She may even experience some ambivalent pleasure because sexuality and emotion are expressed rather than repressed. When the sex offense is exposed, the sexual and emotional expression, together with the offense, upsets the family so that its members overreact by asking questions that the child cannot and should not answer. Or the family may become very worried, overprotective, and extremely comforting, but from a controlled and rigid distance. Such a child could be seriously traumatized and have permanent guilt because of the parent's reactions and because of the conflict between sexual expression and repression. If a child is in a healthy rather than a mad family situation, such a sex offense can usually be accepted and worked out. For instance, the child should be comforted, asked what happened, listened to, and then given calm and appropriate direction. In this healthy situation, the child is more likely to learn from and spontaneously forget the experience.

Incest

Incest is one of the strongest taboos. Although incestuous genital intercourse is relatively rare, it causes and is the result of serious problems. A more frequent and subtle form of incest occurs when a parent fondles a child sexually, as when a father caresses his child's genitals and has the child caress him. Here, the family situation is often repressive and not sexually healthy, and, besides, the father often feels castrated, resentful toward women, and lacks healthy intimate relations with his wife. When the father molests his daughter, which often occurs when he is lonely or depressed, his actions may be an attempt to get close to his daughter, to feel like a man, to get back at women, and/or to fulfull himself sexually.

Although an incestuous act may occur only once or twice, and though the experience may be the closest the father and daughter have been to each other, the daughter is often seriously hurt. She may feel ambivalent, guilty, and develop a resentment toward men. On the one hand, she may have felt close to her father, an experience that seldom if ever had happened before. On the other hand, she may have felt ashamed, afraid, used, and angry. She can easily learn to hate her father and perhaps all men as a way of controlling her mixed feelings. Her goal should be to gain insight into her feelings and to try to understand that her experience may have been part of larger family problems, such as the father-mother relationship and lack of family intimacy. Especially when a person is young, it is very difficult to gain such understanding and to cope constructively without professional help. In time and with competent help, a violated woman can come to accept and perhaps be compassionate toward her father who did more than fondle her.

Abnormal sex offenders are usually men; seldom are women incarcerated or talked about as "sex offenders." Still, women do offend against sex, but their behavior is usually not as overt or as socially offensive as men's. For instance, a mother who sleeps with her thirteen-year-old boy, who parades almost nude in front of her teenage boy, or who wrestles intimately with her eighteen-year-old may be a sex offender. Her unconscious motivations may include resentment toward her husband, controlling men, and being safely sexual. Possible results are that a boy may be frightened and bear resentment toward his mother and women in general, or he may become overly involved with her and eventually marry a woman who represents his mother.

Rape

One definition of a rapist is an abnormal sadist who takes victims by force. Within a psychoanalytic framework, the rapist is counterphobic: he attacks what he really fears—women. Genital rape takes place when a person forces genital sex on another. Such rape is not only a sexual offense but is more deeply a human offense that degrades and insults the integrity and dignity of women. Rape can also be seen as a strategy to prostrate women, to keep them lower than men, so that men have the illusion of being superior.

Still, there can be an understanding of rape, though it is never healthy or good. The rapist is often afraid, resentful, and inadequate with people, especially women. His forceful entry can be a relatively safe way for him to have quasi-intimacy and to compensate for feelings of inferiority. What the rapist often wants deep within himself is some form of genuine contact, but he feels so frightened, intimidated, and angry that he is compelled to stay on top of women. To be sure, rape is the most violent and insulting sex offense.

Rape is not only a matter of concern for celibates, for rape may occur more frequently within marriage than outside it. In fact, some people may remain celibate to prevent marital rape. Some women, for example, would rather remain celibate than be treated unequally and without respect. When a woman is expected to be on constant sexual call, to be always willing and ready to satisfy a man's needs, and "gratefully" to be a sperm receptacle, she is being raped. When sex is not freely experienced, rape is committed. Perhaps rape is more normal than we think.

CHAPTER **VIII**

Sexual Emergence Throughout the Life Cycle

Life is a dynamic process that is continually unfolding. Although we may try to be merely content or to stop change, we are restive and restless—always yearning for deeper meaning and fulfillment. At the moment of conception, we are thrown into the process of the life cycle of birth and death. Dying a meaningful death and creating a more meaningful future is the call to a healthy presence.

Certain stages of development can be charted throughout life. Although these stages are much less precise in the later years than in the early ones, critical periods, moments of adjustment, and times of confrontation can be normatively sketched. Even though these stages and phases of growth may not fit any of us perfectly, they can serve as milestones along life's journey.

Being an integral part of human existence, sexuality can also be part of the life cycle of birth and death. Sexuality can change throughout life according to our situation, stage of growth, psychosocial expectation, and health. The present task is to explore and analyze sexuality throughout the life cycle and discuss some of the obstacles and opportunities that often occur in various developmental stages. A main principle is that sexual development is basically sequential so that each stage builds on previous stages. So if one phase of development is not worked through in a healthy way, later stages can be negatively influenced. We will sketch the development of sexuality in infancy, childhood, and adolescence, and focus on the emergence of primary, genital, and affective sexuality in the adult.

INFANCY AND CHILDHOOD

Despite scientific evidence, some of us still have difficulty in admitting that sexuality exists in infancy and childhood. To consider little people as sexual seems to some to be almost perverse; most of us, however, will admit that primary sexuality is a factor very early in life. We can see that a boy and a girl differ not only in their embodiment but also in how they act and are treated. Our mode of interaction and role expectations differ according to the sexes. If we are unaware of such childhood sexuality, we can impede healthy primary sexual development—an integral part of infancy and childhood.

Affective sexuality also exists in early development. How a boy and girl learn to behave and express themselves often involves affective sexuality. For instance, how close children get to their parents and others varies considerably within different families. Some children learn that the only feeling they can express is anger which is then angrily punished. The expression of affection, care, and intimacy is often curbed and sometimes repressed. To hold, caress, or to kiss a child after he or she is five years old may be taboo, more often for boys than for girls. How parents and others respond to a child's affective sexuality and the kind of sexual differentiations they make toward boys and girls can strongly influence later development.

It may be most difficult for us to admit that little people

have genital experiences. A difficulty may be that we adults tend to project our own standards and experiences of sexuality onto children and consequently make the assumption that genital play means the same to children as it does to us. Since this would not make much sense, we then might conclude that there cannot be any genital sexuality in children. Still, it is consistently and commonly observed that children do engage in genital play. Unlike adult play, childhood genital play is centered around exploration, curiosity, and self-satisfaction. And instead of being oriented toward others or toward genital intercourse, pleasure is self-centered. In this sense, childhood sexuality is "narcissistic" for it involves self-exploration rather than social interaction.

When children play with their genitals or begin to explore the genitals of a brother or sister, they experience a pleasure similar to but different from playing with other bodily parts. To explore private parts may also be exciting. How parents respond to such exploration can be critical to a child's sexual development. Let us look at some of these stages of development in reference to sexuality.

We enter a world we do not choose and which is embedded with certain cultural and subcultural expectations. Every milieu assumes ways of responding to male and female infants. What are our assumptions? Do we harbor any sexist prejudices? Does the mother behave differently toward male and female infants, and if so, how? How does the father feel about the male and about the female child? Does the father take an active part in playing with his child? Does the neonate experience intimacy with the father as well as with the mother? For instance, if the father is a phantom father, the child at this early stage of development may not experience affective sexuality with a man. Whatever the case, all infants find themselves in a situation that is both positive and negative.

Think of the world of infancy. Experience is almost entirely in and through one's own and the bodies of others. Infants have a pure but surface presence to reality. Rational and functional powers are minimal at this time, and spiritual experiences are also latently present.

Initially, bodily contact is centered around the mouth. At first, this oral approach to the world is receptive and incorporative; a little later, it becomes more aggressive. Infants initially are given or receive love, and later begin to take love. Erikson analyzes this first experience of reality in terms of whether or not an infant can trust the world.[1]

We can question the experiences of infancy. Could I depend on the world? Was someone there when needed? Could I freely relax and be at home in the world? Or did I experience an inconsistent and precarious world, one to be careful and wary of? Was I born anxiously on edge, never quite sure of what was going to happen next? Did I feel starved and satiated, or comfortable and fulfilled?

These kinds of critical issues along with the accent of embodied communication can have a significant influence on sexual development. Did I feel at home in the arms of my parents? Did my parents hold me in a rigid and impersonal way, or were they highly anxious and tended to smother me? If bodily contact meant suffocation or starvation, a shaky foundation may have been built—a reluctance to engage in intimacy. Did I begin to learn that affection and human touch are good and comfortable experiences? Did I receive embodied affection solidly and tenderly?

Our first year of life can have a significant impact on our later experiences of sexual development. If as an infant, for example, I was satiated in the first and later years, I could learn to be too dependent on affection including affective sexuality. If frustrated or starved in these initial months, I could grow to be an adult who constantly seeks affective

---

1. E. Erikson, *Identity: Youth and Crisis* (New York: N.W. Norton & Co. Inc., 1968) pp. 96-107.

and sexual reassurance. Or I could learn to grow up to distrust the world because my world was initially unfair and painful.

Around the second year of life, infants begin to test the limits of reality and feel pressures to control their limits. When they respond in ways that please their parents, they are rewarded, and they are more or less punished when these expectations are transgressed. Their senses and understanding are developing along with motor skills, and speech is probably beginning. In other words, they are learning to control themselves and the world. Erikson sees this time as a crisis of autonomy.[2] Can a baby, for example, begin to take some responsibility for behavior, take a stand and regulate life? Or on the other hand, does the infant begin to doubt himself and feel ashamed? Does he begin to compulsively hold onto things because of a lack of autonomy in doubting everything?

A key area, though not the only one, is toilet training, which can often involve implicit attitudes toward sexuality and intimacy. How did our parents respond when cleaning our genitals? Their response to toilet training and genital play also has an impact on the infrastructure of our sexual development.

Already in these first two years sexual roles can be differentiated. Is the baby, male or female, directed to certain kinds of play? Is a boy allowed to play with a doll, or a girl with what is regarded as a boy's toy? Sexual role differentiation may not be very strong at this time, but it can begin in subtle and important ways. Soon after, in the third or fourth year, this sexual differentiation usually becomes clear and strong.

By the third year of life, visual-motor coordination is much better, and speech and comprehension are rapidly

---

2. Ibid. pp. 107-14.

developing. Sexual distinctions also become clear and more complex. Awareness of others becomes more acute and differentiated, and though interpersonal relationships tend to be self-centered and simple, they are nevertheless taking place. These young children begin to move out toward both sexes and often times behave differently toward each. Often the boy will take a special interest in the female, and the girl in the man. Such sexual differentiation occurs early, but it becomes more apparent around the fourth year of life. Of course, this is a two-way street. Often the girl becomes daddy's little girl not only because the girl responds differently to daddy than to mommy, but also because daddy responds differently to his daughter than to his son. Likewise, the mother's attitudes toward the boy may be somewhat different from her attitudes toward the girl. This is not to say that these attitudes are wrong, but that they are different and that the parents should be aware of them.

Erikson describes this crisis as a time of initiative versus guilt.[3] He analyzes the boy's modality of initiative as being on the make, suggesting pleasure in attack and conquest, and he describes the girl's mode of initiative mainly in terms of catching.[4] There may be truth to this model of behavior, for it is common to see a little boy being aggressive and a little girl being seductive. And some biologists say that there are hormonal differences that can predispose a boy to being more aggressive. This is not to say, however, that sexual differences are entirely innate. Parents respond differently to the sexes, and their role expectations influence the way the boy or girl learns to behave.

How our parents respond to us at this time can influence our primary sexual development along with our affective and genital growth. Important influences center around the

---

3. Ibid., pp. 115-22.
4. Ibid., pp. 118.

following issues: Was my father around to serve as a model? And if he was around, how did he interact with me? What was the role of my father in the family? Was he the ultimate authority who was somewhat impersonal and who seldom involved himself with his children? Or did he become a passive person who abdicated his responsibility so that his wife was forced to take more than her share? Was my mother a docile person who found her identity through her husband? Did she harbor resentment? Was she an autonomous person? What were her role expectations of the sexes? What role models did I see at this early stage of development? How we experienced our parents and their expectations have a decided impact on what kind of men and women we develop into.

Such influences may be seen more clearly in the realm of relaxation. What kind of books were read to us? So often, children's books tend to be subtly sexist. For example, boys and male animals tend to be at the center of action where they are usually depicted as aggressive, powerful, and as the most prestigious. But females are passively on the periphery of the action or docilely in service of males. Already as children, we may have been exposed to possible sexist attitudes that have planted questionable seeds for one-sided growth.

This particular stage is especially important for developing initiative and assertiveness. How others, especially our parents, treated us at this time is likely to influence our present attitude toward people and especially those with whom we are intimate. Of course, this stage like other stages is influenced by how trusting and autonomous we already are. If we distrust and feel doubt and shame, we can hardly take an authentic initiative.

We can ask more specific questions. Does a girl at this time begin to learn to be docile or does she learn that her initiative is secondary to men's? Does she begin to learn that a boy can be more assertive? Or conversely, does the boy feel pressured to be aggressive? Does he feel impeded in being tender and affectionate? Boys at this early stage of development can be judged to be backward or even retarded when they are affectionate and tender. (They are expected to act aggressively and roughly.) Our culture tends to see such affectionate behavior as more appropriate for a girl than for a boy. Once again these sexual roles can be questioned.

When we go to school we begin to discover the rest of the world in a new way. Suddenly our world broadens. We are no longer so concerned with ourselves and with our immediate environment. The discovery of our intrapersonal self is no longer as important, and sex is relatively latent. Now we encounter peers, adults, ideas, and ethnic and ethical approaches that are new and different.

Often the elements of competition and comparison influence our interpersonal contacts, and our interest tends to be rooted in the likes and dislikes of self and others. Erikson calls this stage one of industry versus inferiority.[5] Crucial issues at this stage of development center on being adequate in terms of dealing with the world or becoming inadequate in coping with the many demands of ordinary living.

Although sexuality can be less of an issue because we are learning to adjust to, and to function in, different situations, sexuality is still present. For instance, how teachers treat and respond to us as boys or girls makes an impact on our primary sexual development. And within the family structure, we can ask how our parents treated us. Often a father will no longer be intimate with his children, especially the male child. Suddenly a boy may be expected to be distant and perhaps to control and hide his feelings. Affective sexu-

---

5. Ibid., pp. 122-28.

ality between a boy and his father is relatively rare in our culture. By the time a boy is five or six or perhaps even earlier, the father may begin to feel uncomfortable in caressing and kissing his son. Furthermore, sexual differentiation in group activity increases at this time. Although within the family and neighborhood situations boys and girls may play together, at school, boys and girls usually separate into their own groups.

Soon after this early school period and during preadolescence, we develop a friendship. Sullivan calls this friend a chum.[6] Finding a chum and sharing in a deeper way are new experiences in coming to know others and ourselves. This period of chumhood also offers possibilities to realize and test basic trust and mistrust, autonomy and doubt, initiative and guilt, industry and inferiority.

In these elementary school years, "puppy love" can emerge. Puppy love can be an expression of affective sexuality in that as young persons we move a bit closer and respond differently to one another. Can a child feel at home with attraction to the other sex in these early years? Does the boy have to be aggressive with peers or feel guilty for not being aggressive? Does the girl have to be docile and suppress assertiveness?

Early sexual development centers around primary and affective sexuality, and genital sexuality is seldom an explicit issue. Still, genital exploration is not rare. Persons of the same or different sexes may explore each other under the guises as being doctor and patient or mommy and daddy. Although such sexual exploration is usually one of curiosity, exploring private areas is not the same as exploring public areas. There can be a sense of secrecy and excitement. Although prepuberty children can rarely experi-

---

6. Harry Stack Sullivan, *Interpersonal Theory of Psychiatry* (New York: W.W. Norton & Co. Inc., 1968), pp. 245-46.

ence genital intercourse or even be inclined to do so, they can fantasize or even try to emulate genital relations. If a child's history has been one of repressing affection, however, the child can feel unnecessary guilt for such genital curiosity and exploration. This is not to say that such genital activity should be encouraged, but that children should not be made to feel unnecessary guilt. Instead of projecting our own standards of sexual behavior onto the child, we should try to understand, set limits, and give guidance.

ADOLESCENCE

Early adolescence can bring sudden physical and psychological changes so that a child may sometimes feel lost or in flux. Young adolescents are often excited and frightened about these changes, and they wonder about how to integrate all these new experiences. The questions of what role I should play and who I am going to become can be critical in adolescence. Erikson sees the crux of this adolescent stage as a crisis of identity versus role confusion.[7]

Erikson also sees this phase of development as a time when "youth" begins.[8] Young adolescents find themselves as members of that contemporary and expanding group called youth—persons who are neither children nor adults. They can experience themselves as being in a quandary— too old to be children and too young to be adults, while they feel urges from within and pressures from others to become sexual adults.

Sexuality is critically important in early adolescence in all its modalities—primary, genital, and affective. Too often sexual changes are identified only as genital changes, and though genitality is important, primary and affective

---

7. Erikson, *Identity: Youth and Crisis*, pp. 128-35.
8. Ibid., pp. 261-63.

sexuality are just as important. Sexual changes, in whatever modality, can be especially confusing because we feel so strange about them, and our feelings are often intense. The adolescent may react with fear and curiosity, with pleasurable attention and embarrassment, or experience urges to share and withdraw. Many adolescents probably feel somewhere in the middle: moving both toward and away from sex.

Although many physical changes in adolescence are explicitly genital, they are interwoven with primary sexuality. Since we are our bodies, bodily changes mean psychological changes. As adolescents, we begin to see ourselves differently, and others begin to respond to us differently.

Cultural expectations influence sexual development during adolescence. Boys want to be taller, stronger, and heavier than they are, and girls usually want to be shorter and lighter. Girls desire smaller hips and waists, thinner arms and legs, and larger breasts; boys seek the cultural stereotype of broader shoulders and thicker arms and legs. Furthermore, boys and girls are naturally and culturally ordered to carry and use their bodies differently. Girls at this time begin to be more graceful, less assertive, and more interpersonally concerned. Boys are often pressured to be more assertive, aggressive, and seem to have more license in being disorderly. Such cultural stereotypes can be questioned.

As we have seen, becoming a man or woman begins very early. How an adolescent was treated as a child has a decided effect on finding a healthy identity. For example, if as a child a girl could only play with dolls, always had to be "nice," and always took second place to men, her adolescent view of becoming an adult woman has already been formed to a large degree. On the other hand, if the female child was allowed to be angry, to stand up for her rights, and do so-called boy's things, she probably will have a different view of being a woman at this critical time.

Adult attitudes conveyed to the adolescent at this time are also critically important. For example, how does a mother or father respond to the female adolescent? Does the mother think that women are just as important as and contribute just as much as men? Does she encourage her adolescent girl to be competent and competitive as well as warm and receptive? Does her father treat her as a fragile piece of glass? Or does he encourage her to strive and succeed as much as her brother? The kind of parents an adolescent has influences the kind of man or woman the adolescent will become. If a mother sells herself short, is docile, or takes second place to men, the adolescent girl will be influenced by this constant behavior. Or on the other hand, if the mother takes pride in who she is, enjoys doing many things, or feels just as worthwhile as a man, her child's view of being a woman will be quite different from the other girl's.

Research reveals that women can be made to feel less valuable than men, can be put and kept in places and roles they do not choose, and can be banned from certain activities. Much of this mad programming is stressed during adolescence. For instance, it seems that as soon as girls begin to look like women, they are pressured to focus on interpersonal relationships or to give up career aspirations. Or they are steered away from certain so-called masculine fields such as engineering, science, and business. A person of either sex should learn interpersonal skills, but not at the expense of giving up career possibilities. Such oppression is not only unjust to the individual but also violates society.

Pressure and role expectations imposed on boys are also vitally important at this time. Boys who are taught in childhood to see girls as weak, passive, fickle, and subservient to men, may realize these attitudes more significantly in adolescence. An adolescent boy may also experience stronger pressure than in his recent past to fulfill questionable roles of masculinity. So-called feminine qualities such as gentleness, sensitivity, and a poetic style are not as acceptable and can easily evoke peer criticism. The stress is more likely to be on qualities such as aggressiveness, competition, physical prowess, emotional control, and "coolness." Especially in adolescence, a boy can be reinforced to hide or repress affectionate feelings behind an aggressive facade.

Too often we can assume that there are huge and clear differences between boys and girls, men and women. Such differences are neither huge nor clear, and certainly they can be questioned. There are no qualities or activities that are in themselves male or female, masculine or feminine. Men and women are two sides of the same coin; one without the other makes little sense. How qualities and activities such as nurturing and assertiveness are expressed may differ somewhat according to the sexes, but these differences should be complementary, not mutually exclusive.

The false assumption often exists that a man's image of sexual identity or of being a man is much clearer and set than a woman's. It may indeed be more set, but not necessarily clearer or healthier. What it means culturally to be a true man is neither unclear nor always best for mental health. If a male adolescent is taught never to show feelings, feel intensely with another, show love, or be tender, his identity is not healthy. If he is taught that it is unmanly to cook, sew, and do housework, he may be impeding his growth.

Actually, a boy is often less certain of his (sexual) identity than an adolescent girl. Often a boy lacks a positive impact from his father, or his father's role model is far from what it should be. Or, if an adolescent boy has a phantom father, his mother can be pressured to fill the gap. In fact, girls sometimes may be more sure of their sexual identity than boys because many mothers spend more time with their children than fathers do. Nevertheless, although a girl may have relative freedom in her childhood, upon reaching adolescence her situation is often oppressive.

In early adolescence, genital sexuality becomes a powerful urge. Unlike genitality in the prepuberty years, genitality now orients us socially so that we begin to explore the possibility of genital relations with others. Genital experiences, however, seldom happen in reality, but more likely in fantasy. Genital fantasies can in some ways help prepare us for later life, though this is not to say that such fantasy should be encouraged or that desires should be satisfied. As presented in our discussion on genital sexuality, our fantasies and feelings should be listened to, understood, and ultimately integrated within our whole personality. Since the attitudes we develop toward genitality at this time can highly influence later development, mere repression or satisfaction can cause future difficulty. The ideal is to promote a chaste attitude toward sexuality especially genitality—to see, listen to, and integrate sexuality.

Chastity can be difficult to achieve at this time, but it is possible. It is difficult because genital feelings are so strong and new and because adolescents are learning to integrate feelings of sexuality. And it is relatively easy to regard genitality as the total experience. Sometimes genitality can be so strong that adolescents seem to become just genital beings. Once caught in a genital world, there seems to be no alternative but satisfaction (usually via masturbation) or frustration. To condemn adolescents or to make them feel guilty is harmful, but our challenge is to help them integrate genitality. Unfortunately, adolescents are given help or questionable help, in terms of satisfaction or repression. Perhaps adolescents could learn that there are other ways besides repression and satisfaction.

A recurrent problem is that many adolescents lack the discipline that is necessary for authentic freedom. Too many adolescents have had a relatively tensionless and frustration-free childhood because all needs and wants have been indiscriminately satisfied. Such well-intentioned spoiling, though seemingly more humane than limited freedom, can easily promote self-centeredness, low frustration tolerance, and a lack of discipline needed for later growth. Furthermore, children and adolescents are too seldom given a point of view or infrequently taught an awareness of, and a responsibility for, right and wrong behavior. Consequently, when their crisis of identity occurs, adolescents may have neither guiding principles nor the discipline to cope with the pain of self-discovery. Thus, they can too easily regress to a narcissistic posture of self-satisfaction, overtly rebel or escape from life's demands, be too influenced by peers and questionable cultural values, or simply live a diffuse and immature life.

Affective sexuality can also be a problem. It is often very difficult for adolescent males to feel tender and considerate, let alone promote these qualities. Such boys may be labeled effeminate and be rejected by many of the boys as well as by many girls. Boys who prefer so-called feminine activities such as music, art, and sewing will probably have a difficult time. Since boys seldom get much help in integrating the female and feminine within themselves, they can easily be taught to deny their existential bisexuality and become one-sidedly masculine.

Likewise, an adolescent female is often impeded in pursuing so-called masculine activities. If a girl wants to study auto mechanics, for example, she is usually persuaded to change her mind, is seen as a "special case," or labeled tomboy and immature. Although some of these sexist differentiations are disappearing, many still do exist. Even though a woman may have relatively more freedom in the way she dresses, the places she frequents, and what she says, she may still be oppressed in terms of her personal, professional, and political freedom. Boys and men "do not mind" girls and women being and acting differently as long as "they stay in their place"—as long as they do not usurp masculine positions and power.

In middle adolescence, around sixteen or seventeen, primary sexuality becomes more settled, even though it may be filled with sexist prejudices. Along with primary sexuality and learning sexual roles, affective sexuality becomes more refined. In fact, affective sexuality can be intense because at this time we often experience a period of romantic idealism—to view life in terms of the ideal. Midadolescent sexuality lends itself to this romantic posture.

By now positive and/or negative ways to cope with genitality have been learned, and though there is often a period of stability around middle adolescence, the expression of genital sexuality becomes much more frequent than some of us realize, although perhaps less frequent than others think. Still, possibilities for interpersonal genital satisfaction are greater. For most midadolescents, masturbation serves as the main source of genital gratification, and it may increase with women who often begin masturbating later than boys.

Opportunities for genital relations, coupled with romantic idealism, can be seductive. Some adolescents may want to give themselves wholly or "perfectly" including genitally. Or they can fool themselves into thinking they have complete control of their sexuality and can therefore express it any way they want. Some may feel they completely own their bodies and can do as they like with themselves. Furthermore, modern technology has made it relatively easy to prevent pregnancy and childbirth.

And yet, it is not rare to see some adolescents become somewhat scrupulous in midadolescence. Judging life in light of the ideal can pressure some (especially those with compulsive tendencies) to be hyperconscious about the morality of feelings and acts. Others, however, affirm and implement healthy attitudes toward sexuality. Adolescents can begin to integrate genitality, promote affective sexuality, and become authentic men and women.

Although all of us experience critical times throughout life, we are likely to keep, though modified and deepened, our adolescent attitudes. Thus, this period that comes before young adulthood is often significant to future sexual development.

YOUNG ADULTHOOD

Late adolescence leads to the threshold of young adulthood—a period of adjustment that centers around changing one's life situation, social roles, and personal identity. Most individuals enter college and/or join the work force, and begin to live in a new situation or stay at home in a new way. Such environmental changes call for personal adjustment, including sexual adjustment.

Consider, for instance, late adolescents who have rigidly controlled or repressed sexuality. If they move away from home, they experience different values and pressures, restrictions and controls are lessened, and new opportunities for sexual satisfaction may emerge. Thus, these novices of adulthood may experience new feelings or old feelings in new ways, and they may be tempted to engage in sexual activities too quickly. Their repressed sexuality may suddenly flood out when they enter new situations.

If young adults have had a childhood history that fostered indulgent and narcissistic behavior rather than disciplined and principled behavior, they may find themselves without guiding standards for healthy behavior and feel under pressure to satisfy rather than integrate their sexuality. Children who are raised to think that all viewpoints are of equal value and who always get what they want can become aimless and egocentric young adults. Though seemingly more open than their predecessors, they also fragment and fail to integrate sex.

Many young adults feel almost guilty for not satisfying their sexual needs—often the opposite of what their parents experienced. Not to satisfy sexuality may be considered a sign of stupidity, puritanism, immaturity, or sickness. Recreational sex is promoted in service of need, satisfaction, fun, and learning. Some think that as long as they are "sincere and honest" they can engage in sexual relations. They fail to realize that sincerity and honesty do not guarantee healthy behavior. Such sexual behavior is neither unhealthy nor healthy but is normal and mad, for ongoing integral growth includes and goes beyond satisfaction and adjustment.

Environmental changes can also affect primary and affective sexuality. For instance, young women or men who are exposed to women's studies may reevaluate their sexual values, roles, and expectations. Or role expectations at work may change significantly from high school days. A woman, for instance, may experience more than before being treated as a sex object, or a man may feel the pressure to manifest a macho facade. Opportunities and pressures in living arrangements, in social and recreational situations, and at work also can bear heavily on sexuality.

Soon after entering this threshold of adulthood, these "young adults" usually experience a personal crisis. Usually around nineteen or twenty and/or not rarely in the mid-twenties, we go through a rather intense period of self-evaluation wherein we are thrown back on ourselves—questioning our values, goals, past inheritance, other persons (especially parents and other significant people), and life in general. Who am I? Whence do I come? Where am I going? All these classical questions become critically important, and initially, few valid answers emerge.

During this novitiate of adulthood, a period of darkness precedes the light of young adulthood; a moratorium comes before a committed life. These young adults often experience intense feelings of loneliness—a yearning to be understood by and to be with another while at the same time feeling empty. The intimate presence of another is experienced more in absence than in presence. This loneliness, however, can be important because it can help us discover ourselves so that ultimately we can surrender ourselves in intimacy. And along with loneliness, we often feel alone—by ourselves but not necessarily yearning for others. Then we can listen to and reflect on life, and hope to find and live our pace and place. At other times, we may feel alone and lonely—silently shouting without any response.

Such loneliness and aloneness can be important experiences in finding ourselves—including our sexual self. Questions about sexuality seek important answers. What kind of a man or woman am I? How can I or should I express my affective sexuality? What is the meaning of genitality in my life? All modes of sexuality can be questioned at this time. And although we can be exposed to, and influenced by, consciousness-raising groups, we are usually unlikely to commit ourselves to such a movement. Our impetus for change at this time is more internal than external, more personal than political. We can, however, reflect on our past and may see sexist influences. For instance, recognizing how we were steered into certain areas without being given a real opportunity to enter into others can evoke anger and frustration. Some of us may repress insight and unknowingly go along with sexist programming. Or we may find such knowledge interesting but not act on it until we have later suffered it. Our sexual search is mainly an interior search to discover ourselves in order to surrender ourselves.

Primary sexuality is radically questioned. What and who is a woman? A man? How do men and women differ? How much and in what way do sexist role expectations influence me? What is the difference between sex versus gender—and how do I integrate them? Who am I sexually? Although we can confront similar issues as adolescents, we usually do not articulate them as clearly and strongly as persons coming to young adulthood. Part of adulthood includes being a mature sexual being. But what is mature sexuality?

Genital sexuality is also a key area in the late teens and early twenties, and the sexual stance we take at this time can be critical to future development. Some repress or delay genitality. Repression at this time, however, may be difficult because normally our social milieu promotes sexual gratification and those who do repress or even suppress sexuality may get a negative feedback. Others may be in a situation that curtails genital opportunities or stimulation. Our environment may even be oppressive and present obstacles that militate against healthy genital integration. For instance, a religious celibate may be in a situation where people tend to disregard genitality and consequently sex is not openly discussed. Of course, not all and not only religious lack genital awareness.

Some young adults simply postpone genital emergence. We can be so busy studying, working, and finding our psychological and spiritual selves that we forget about sexuality. Although such postponement is not the same as repression, it is not a way to work through and to integrate genitality. If we postpone (or repress) sexuality, we will be confronted later in life with experiences that we should have faced up to earlier. If earlier stages of sexual growth development are repressed, postponed, or blatantly satisfied, later stages of sexual growth can be adversely affected.

Although postponement and repression do occur, there are more opportunities and expectations that celibates will engage in genital sexuality. To be a twenty-one-year-old celibate is not usually a popular situation and semi-social sanctions may even punish persons for being celibate. Perhaps more for men than for women, celibacy is often something to hide rather than proclaim. Men as well as women may snicker at a celibate young man, or they may wonder if he is homosexual or unhealthy. Social expectations encourage genital behavior as part of being a normal adult.

Genital relations can be seductive not only because of social expectations but also because of the painful experiences of self-discovery. Genital satisfaction, as we have seen, offers pleasure, some ecstasy, and temporary fulfillment. If we feel lonely, alone, and depressed, sometimes any-body may seem better than no-body. Although genital pleasure can be an accessible way to purge pain, it can also be a way of running from oneself in the guise of meeting self and another. We have also seen that genital behavior in and of itself does not promote healthy growth. Furthermore, since healthy loneliness, depression, and other pain involved in self-discovery are seldom socially sanctioned and are often seen as indicative of something wrong instead of as necessary for growth, we can be pressured to escape from or numb such pain by engaging in genital relations. Consequently, in service of normality, we can escape from ourselves and impede our growth.

Young adults have many opportunities to test the limits and possibilities of affective sexuality. Young celibates, including religious, have more opportunity and encouragment to share and to promote intimacy. Learning ways to function and how to be affectionate with others are significant issues. Questioning our bisexuality, we may see the influences of gender and of learning on our affective sexuality. A young man may ask himself if it is necessary to hide feelings, or if it is possible to be emotionally expressive and genuinely gentle. A young woman may wonder if it is necessary to be submissive, and, upon reflecting on how she can be assertive, she may experience strong feelings to speak out rather than to suffer silently. These young celibates are likely to search their values and later test them in the cultural mainstream.

This phase of development in the beginning years of young adulthood is one of self-discovery that is basically in service of self-implementation and self-surrender. Ideally, as young adults we come to face our sexuality in all its dimensions and formulate deep sexual values that will carry us through life. If for whatever reason we fail to learn in this period of self-discovery, our sexual values and identity will be precarious. At this time, sexual identity and growth, though always unfolding, are crucial for later development.

The middle phase of young adulthood usually occurs in our twenties and primarily involves the challenge to implement the values we have discovered in the earlier years of young adulthood. We enter the world at large to find our personal and professional vocation. Being a "legal adult" can open up opportunities on all levels including sexual ones. Freedom—from parental and environmental restraints and freedom for whatever we choose—is greater at this time. The challenge to implement our sexual self then becomes a developmental task.

In the twenties, sex roles often become more stabilized and explicit. For instance, so-called masculine supremacy in the worlds of work and politics can be taken for granted or tolerated. A man may be under pressure to adopt sexist roles, and a woman will be expected to accept these roles. Women may also be pressured to be in the home; otherwise, women are given secondary positions. Masculine models of supremacy, activity, and authority may contrast with feminine models of being other-oriented, home-centered, and less significant. Some women passively accept such roles, while others may freely accept some of them and reject others. Some protest radically. Expectations of how to be accountable, to earn a living, to take care of others, and to enjoy life are often differentiated according to sexist roles.

The pressures to be contemporary or "cool" often impede healthy sexual integration. And yet when we commit ourselves to a vocation, our approval of premarital sex is likely to drop sharply. Perhaps we become more sensitive to the whole person and consequently are less likely to see others as despiritualized bodies or as sex objects. It seems that when we try to live only for momentary gratification we are less likely to grow in depth and permanence.

ADULTHOOD

Around the age of twenty-nine we usually go through another period of adjustment, and though we do not find ourselves in a deep crisis, we often look at ourselves a bit differently as we approach thirty. A woman may reflect on and wonder what has happened to her sexual life in the last ten years. She may wonder if her celibate dreams, honeymoon ideals, or marital goals have been fulfilled. Celibates may look at themselves and wonder where their sexuality has gone, or they may experience a new and powerful surge of sexuality. We begin to realize that we are no longer young adults but are becoming older. This adjustment is usually a prelude for another crisis in adulthood.

The crisis of adulthood most often occurs in the thirties.

Another reevaluation process takes place—and personal and professional commitments in particular are evaluated. We realize that whatever we need or want, we had better do it now because later it may be much more difficult or practically impossible to realize.

Classic questions emerge again. Where have I been? What have I done? What is the best I can do? Have I grown older together in love with my spouse? Or, will I ever get married? Do I want to get married? The vowed celibate might ask: Is this the right life for me? How spiritual am I really? Do I know what it means to love and to be loved? If I wait another ten years, what options will I really have? Do I want to be a lay person? Married? How possible is marriage? Questions persist with few answers. Do I want to live the rest of my life the way I have been living? Is there more to life? Is this all there is?

Often at this time women can become acutely aware of their relative lack of freedom. They may question their lives and search for more self-expansion, and they are more likely than previously to fight for their rights. They also reflect on their own values and may confront unresolved issues like low self-esteem and insecurity. If they have had some power in their personal and professional lives, they are unlikely to settle for less than the best. In short, past and present sex roles, cultural prejudices, double standards, and personal attitudes are questioned. Some women escape from this crisis through alcoholism, motherism, careerism, or simply withdraw into emotional isolation. Others can break down because of environmental and personal stress. Still others break through to fuller self-realization and happiness.

Women often reach their sexual peak in their thirties and forties, and because of physical and psychological freedom and more social and personal awareness, they can actualize themselves more fully and function more assertively and autonomously. They may also become more sophisticated and effectively sexual, and genitality increases and seeks deeper satisfaction and fulfillment—more and better embodied love.

Men, however, are often too busy to cultivate their sexuality, and this failure can cause intrapersonal and interpersonal conflict. To compensate for their sexual fixation (or lack of growth), men may have quick "physical" sex instead of integral sex. Women who are more in tune with the spirituality of sexuality can intimidate men who take sexuality simply as a means of pleasure. To demand more than the physical—to ask also for love and to expect love to be concretely shown in daily living can indict the unauthentic lives of many men. Women's assertiveness and personal and social awareness can also intimidate men, and men may defend themselves against women by forcing them to be more submissive than ever. Furthermore, men may not be nearly as sexual as women at this time, not only genitally but also existentially and effectively. Without knowing it, women may have surpassed men in sexual as well as overall development. In a culture that proposes men as the vanguards of sexuality, especially of genitality, men can easily be threatened by women who are more sexual than they are. Men may feel socially and personally castrated.

This can also be a ripe time for an affair, for in our thirties we can minimize the sense and fulfillment and maximize the madness and frustration of our lives. We are still young enough to get around and old enough to know how to get around, and if we are going to make a move, this is the time to make it. If we are celibates, we may reflect on our lives and wonder where the past ten years have gone. We may wonder if we really want to get married, and if so, how to go about it without demeaning ourselves. Although we may want to be married, we can become disenchanted when we look at all the marriages that are normally mad.

Celibate women may become aware of the many married men who are "willing" to enter a relationship with them. They may observe how easy it can be to enter such a temporary relationship but wonder if it is adequate or the best possible way. Celibate men can see the many married women who are lonely, frustrated, and perhaps prime for an affair. But celibates, especially women, often question the future security and fulfillment of such arrangements.

Consider religious celibates at this time. If their lives have been only matters of adjustment and functional success and have been lacking in personal growth and spiritual meaning, they may seriously question if the religious life is right for them. They may find that what they thought they committed themselves to—the religious life—is missing. Instead of spiritual people, they may have become successful functionaries. And if a religious, especially a woman, is called to get married, she had better leave her community now. She will discover considerable difficulty in getting married in her thirties, and extreme difficulty later on.

As we have said, whether celibate or married, women usually reach their genital peak around this time. Aside from curiosity, the search for affirmation as a female person along with an intense loneliness can pressure a celibate woman into sexual relationships. The realization that she will never know and give to and receive from a man in genital intimacy can evoke burning frustration and emptiness. When a woman feels that she has much to give and no one to give to, sometimes any man seems better than no man. Generally, a man has more choice between either a younger or an older women in contrast to a woman who must choose a man of the same age or older.

When we are no longer young adults, we begin to see through sexual myths. We see that sexuality is not all ecstasy or a panacea for life's problems. Dreams vanish to be replaced by stark reality. The frustration of a less than fulfilling life, the loneliness of absent love, and the feeling that time is running out may motivate us to enter genital relationships.

This can also be a time to reaffirm, rekindle, modify, or nourish sexuality, and an excellent time to integrate sexuality and spirituality. Celibates may become more sensitive to the interrelationship of love and sexuality and to the relational character of sexuality rather than focusing merely on its pleasurable and reproductive dimensions. As we grow older, we can see and experience the whole beings of others and are less likely to focus only on their periphery. We can experience the spiritual and aesthetic, not only the functional or physical. Celibate life can become intensely and wholly sexual. Instead of being a source of painful frustration, genitality can promote vitality and spirituality. Celibates can become, more than ever, vital lovers.

Married people may also enjoy sex more than ever, especially if they have actively promoted their spiritual lives. The man can learn from the woman and the woman from the man. For instance, the man can be careful not to become a workaholic and therefore be too tired and preoccupied for healthy sexuality. He can be careful to stay in good physical and spiritual shape so he can engage more freely in sexual relationships. The woman can initiate loving sex and manifest herself as a woman of worth. Both can experience the power of sexual transcendence.

If sexual awareness and expression have been repressed or postponed, sexuality can explode in one's thirties. If a lid has been put on sexuality, the lid is likely to come off at this time. (This sexual explosion can be postponed indefinitely or into the late thirties or forties.) When repressed or postponed sexuality begins to emerge, it is usually very difficult to integrate and to make it meaningful. Although we may be or appear to be adult in most areas, we can behave like adolescents in our naive and giddy approach to sexuality.

If we have repressed or postponed sexuality, we may be too giddy or play "touchy-touchy, tickle-tickle" games. Of course, we can be giddy, childish, or adolescent at times, but when such behavior is frequent and intense, it is not healthy or mature. If we move from repression or postponement to explosion, we can be easily seduced. Unknowingly, we can be prime candidates for sexual games. A man who is sensitive to moral or spiritual values can easily seduce a woman who has repressed or postponed her sexuality. If he promises love and shows some concern and interest for her as a human being, she may be more likely to give herself genitally. This naive woman can be deeply hurt because of her vulnerability in looking for caring while she is used only as a genital being. Or he may use the "line" that it is all right if she abstains from genital intercourse for he "accepts" her. He plays on the woman's guilt, betting that she will soon succumb to his "unselfish and sacrificial care."

Consider a man who has never really been open to or has tried to integrate his sexuality until his thirties. His world may sometimes become "sexualized," or he may feel strong urges to be intimate. But since he probably does not know how to integrate and manifest sexuality, he may become angry at and embarrassed with himself. Though he functions well in other areas, he has sexual problems. When affective and genital sexuality emerge, he may become confused or attempt to satisfy himself blatantly. His challenge is to work through his past attitudes and restricted experiences to come to a better sexual stand.

Religious who have postponed or repressed genitality can experience a crisis of commitment. Religious can easily misinterpret their new genital emergence (which is often coupled with lonely emptiness) as a message to leave religious life. They can delude themselves into feeling that genital gratification and/or marriage is necessary for happiness, and consequently think they have no religious vocation. Religious should not become lay people because of genital frustration and loneliness but only because they can be better committed lovers. Frustration and loneliness should not be primary motivations for entering any experience, including marriage. We should try to wait until we are more settled and at home with ourselves, until we have made sense of our loneliness and integrated our genitality, before we make any radical decision.

If, at this time, we come to a mature sexual integration, we really begin to experience authentic manhood or womanhood. We become mature adults—spiritual persons who are sexual. Our sexuality is integrated with our functionality and spirituality, and we feel at home with ourselves and others. We feel the autonomy and solidarity of being mature men and women.

Sexual relations with others as celibate (or married) persons become more natural and meaningful. Affective sexuality can be seen as an end in itself and not necessarily as leading to genitality. We can read our own motivations and the motivations of others in homo- and heterosexual relations. Becoming much more aware of our sexual selves enables us to become aware of the sexuality of others, and consequently less likely to be seduced or to play sexual games. A healthy stand toward sexuality is promoted— sexuality is integrated with the psychological and spiritual. Although sexual growth never ends, we feel that we are really becoming sexual adults.

MIDLIFE ADULTHOOD

Like the earlier stages and phases of development, there is a cyclic rhythm in midlife. Around thirty-nine a period of adjustment often takes place—a transition from adulthood to midadulthood. Forty is not exactly old, but for most of us it is past the halfway point in life which can evoke new role expectations. For instance, though women are still at their sexual peak and their genitality may even increase at this time, they may be under pressure to be nonsexual. The culture's adoration of youth can force midlifers to minimize sex and result in frustration. Men, more often than women, can sublimate their sexual energy in work and can satisfy their genital needs via masturbation, prostitution, or recreational sex. Women, however, usually feel the pain of sexual frustration more than men, yet, because of their primary sexuality and because of cultural influences, women are not as prone to cope with genitality in unauthentic ways.

A woman in her forties can intimidate men because of her sexual development. Indeed, her demands are usually not unjust, but she expects more and can give more than most men. By midlife, a woman has often learned to be more assertive and autonomous, thus she is less likely to accept or condone sexual oppression, shallow sex, or less than is really possible. Of course, some women allow men to think they (men) are supreme and satisfactory, but subtle power may exist in "allowing" men to delude themselves.

Perhaps her most significant power and consequent threat to men lies not as much in what a woman does as in who she is. For instance, she is less likely than the man to dissociate genitality from the whole person or to become fixated on function. Furthermore, a woman is more likely to promote such spiritual qualities as care and compassion. Unfortunately, too many women minimize their spiritual power and compromise themselves by focusing on, and striving for, the physical and functional power of men. Women may also threaten men genitally, men who are inadequate because they eat, drink, and work too much and are, as a result, out of shape, tense, and preoccupied. Thus, men may want infrequent and quick sex—a form of impotence—or have an extramarital affair to hide their tenuous masculinity. Such an affair will often be with a young woman who is also searching for her (sexual) identity so that the man feels less intimidated and has the illusion of sexual potency.

In marriage, if a man and woman have simply learned to adjust to each other instead of growing older together in love, their sex often may be infrequent and perfunctory. If they have not grown in spirituality along with their sexuality, their genital experiences are only physical and consequently become boring. Many couples in midlife feel sexual but do not know how to express their sexuality, for they have come to be sexual strangers. If this has happened, the pressure for an extramarital affair is not rare. A man who begins to feel older often may try to look and act younger, to be a Don Juan. Women may ridicule or exploit him, but some may be seduced by his fatherly or youthful pretense. In any case, there is little integration of sexuality and spirituality because of past fixation and a lack of preparation for midlife.

Whether in lay or religious celibacy or in marriage, men and women are too often far from sexual synchrony. As we have seen, this disharmony not only causes genital problems but also primary and affective sexual difficulties and consequently an overall violation of personal growth and maturity. Perhaps male religious are more likely to resemble women's patterns of sexual growth than those of laymen. Because of the spiritual and psychological formation and style of living of male religious, sexuality may become a critical issue in midlife or sooner. Rather than in their late teens and twenties, religious may reach their genital peak in their thirties and forties.

In the midlife crisis, we go through periods of depression and self-criticism. We experience life in terms of its limits, and we may wonder where the meaning of life has gone even if life has been essentially good. If we live through this crisis of limits in a healthy way, we come to experience life no longer as meaningless but as meaningful and worthwhile.

This is often a critical time of readjustment in assessing our life of love. We may strengthen and deepen our love, or we may take stock of our past love and feel insecure about our future. Or we simply adjust to each other's independence and go our own exclusive ways, and though we may give the minimum of love, we do not actively promote a life of love. Consequently, we fall out of love.

Celibates also reassess their life of love. If a celibate is ever going to get married, this may be the last chance. We begin to feel older and women especially experience relatively few opportunities for marriage. Vowed celibates may also reflect on their life of love and sometimes wonder if they have chosen the right vocation. Sexuality and a yearning for love may be intense, and when genital sexuality and loneliness combine, frustration and pressure can be intense. Such celibates may wonder if they ought to go through life without ever having been genitally intimate.

Celibates can have a difficult time. A woman in her late thirties or early forties may feel intensely sexual and not know what to do. Empty and debilitating frustration can permeate her life, and though she may periodically indulge in masturbation or genital relations with another, she is still frustrated. Her fleeting sexual experiences may give her some temporary satisfaction but eventually leave her yearning for genital-spiritual fulfillment.

Or consider the religious sister who has become conscious of her sexuality in her late thirties and is at her peak in her forties. Perhaps she has not repressed sexuality but has never had the opportunity to discover her sexual self, and now for the first time she explicitly yearns to be intimate with a man. Perhaps she has had very little heterosexual closeness in her childhood and adolescence, that is, a relationship with a man (including her father) has been radically missing. Now she feels emptiness intensely. Her loneliness cries out for intimacy. This sister could mistake her sexual emergence for a lack of vocation—thinking that her yearnings to be intimate can only be met in genital relations. Usually such a woman seeks love along with genital intimacy and thus may desire marriage. Still, she knows that if she leaves religious life, marriage or meeting an adequate male is unlikely at her age. There are probably few available men who could equal her psychological, intellectual, and spiritual levels. Thus, her frustration can be intense, and she can feel hopelessly trapped.

It may be tempting but frightening to leave the community, and frustrating but secure to stay in religious life. Ideally, any decision should be postponed until the person feels more settled. If such feelings as loneliness and sexual frustration are not fundamentally resolved, the prognosis is guarded. Celibates with personal problems are likely to have more problems as lay or married people. And yet staying in religious life can be safer not necessarily better. Nevertheless, it is possible to strengthen and improve religious life in and through this crisis so that staying in the community may be the best way. The goal is to choose *freely* the vocation that promotes the best love and happiness for self and others.

MIDDLE AGE

The age of fifty usually marks another transition—from the midlife to middle age—that leads to the crisis of middle age. Another period of self-confrontation and reevaluation emerges, and sexuality is also questioned. We are likely to confront ourselves again—to question our values even though we have lived them for more than half a lifetime.

What does it mean to be a man or woman? Interpersonal relations or the lack of them are also radically questioned and evaluated.

We may feel unloved even though we may know that love exists. Although our head knows that love is present, our heart feels emptiness. Sometimes we may try to have a promiscuous affair to fill our empty heart, or, because of lack of enthusiasm, we may become overinvolved in genitality and therefore run from the true source of enthusiasm—spirituality. In this dark night, there is often a search for transcendent love—a love that goes beyond life's vicissitudes to the permanence of life.

This dark night of the soul will lead to light, we hope, but while we are in darkness, we can feel anxiously empty and depressed. We are experiencing a most important truth—that we are past the halfway mark in life and therefore closer to death than to life. The voice of death calls for self-assessment which includes sexual assessment.

Under the pressure of feelings such as depression, anxiety, and alienation, sexuality may seem to be a mute question. The vitality and excitement of sexuality may seem contrary to these apparently deadening feelings. Yet, sexuality at this time is a critical challenge. Can middle-aged persons really reevaluate their sexuality and still nourish themselves sexually? It is all to easy to withdraw from sexual discovery and encounter. Studies indicate that the way we deal with sexuality at this time has a strong influence on our future sexual lives. If sexuality is maintained and nourished, the prognosis is much better for an active and meaningful sexual life.

Sexual questions emerge: Am I a man? A woman? Have I been in my past life? Have I lived an authentic sexual life not only genitally but also existentially? Will I be a sexual being in the future? Have I really experienced sexuality in depth? Will I ever enjoy genital sex again? Have I missed sexual experiences that can no longer be experienced?

Both men and women can too easily become "sexless" especially genitally and affectively and thus existentially. Many men continue their sexual atrophy, perhaps with some episodic genital sprees at their convenience. Though some men feel freer to be more affective, too many stifle their affection. Consequently, they become less than integral men.

As Paula Weidegger poignantly points out, middle-aged women can easily become sexually invisible not because of constitutional factors but because of sexist expectation.[1] She shows how many women, including proponents of women's liberation, accept a male definition of menopause—a uniquely female experience. Women can be led to believe that menopause is a sexual disaster rather than a uniquely female opportunity to be different and equal. Instead of becoming more sexual than ever, women may tragically accept the violent and false diagnosis of "change of life"—from being sexual to being neuter.

We can easily doubt our sexual appeal. "Am I really attractive?" can become a significant question. But what is attractiveness? Sexual appeal? Masculinity? Femininity? If we see attractiveness as a manifestation of spiritual and psychological embodiment, then attractiveness can take on a deeper meaning. But if we have focused only on physical expression and appearance, then we can easily regress. We can play sad charades of youth. For instance, a man may dress like a young adult and try to perform activities characteristic of young adults. A woman may suddenly begin to look like her daughter and/or students and become a sad caricature of what she is futilely striving for.

Because of physical, psychological, and spiritual changes,

---

1. Paula Weidegger *(Menstruation and Menopause)* New York: Dell Publishing Co., 1977).

genital sex may be relatively minimal. It is important to realize, however, that genital and overall life at this time highly influences future sexual life. The stand we take toward primary sexuality influences significantly our sexual stand for the remainder of our adult life. And if genitality is not integrated at this time, it can slowly disintegrate and atrophy.

Important is the attitude we have taken toward ourself and others. If we have responded only to the physical side of ourselves and others, then our shallow sexual stand usually catches up with us at this time. No longer can we play such sexual games, but are finally caught in our mad stand. If we have seen sexuality merely as a quantitative game rather than a qualitative relationship, sexuality is dissipated. The monotony of repetitious and purely physical sex becomes a boring routine. Too many men become preoccupied with their careers and economic pursuits so they neither involve themselves freely nor have the energy and interest to promote healthy, especially affective, sexual relations. Again, at this time, mental and physical fatigue, along with overindulgence in food and drink, can also contribute to sexual inadequacies.

In middle age, our bisexuality is more likely to emerge and can be clearly realized. Can a man learn to integrate so-called feminine characteristics so that he becomes more wholly bisexual in his manly way? Can he really begin to learn to nourish ways of being gentle, sensitive, and poetic? Can a woman become more assertive, independent, and rational; that is, engage in more so-called masculine activities? Healthy people who emerge out of this crisis of middle age do become more whole—women become more like men and men become more like women. Each sex takes on more of the qualities and activities of the other sex. The sexes become more whole and alike. But this can be especially problematic for a man if he has repressed so-called feminine attributes. Still, as a man becomes older he often feels freer to give up his sexual one-sidedness; he feels less need to play sexual games and finds little reason to use sexist power. He can feel more secure in accepting and integrating his other half.

In the later phases of the middle years, in the fifties and sixties, sexuality can be quite active. Although genital activity may not be as frequent as it was in the past, the qualitative residue may be greater. That is, the increase in quality can lessen a need for quantity. An important factor in late middle age is our past sexual life. If sexuality has been inactive, or not integrated, then the prognosis for a healthy sexual life in late middle age and the elderly years is poor. If sexuality has been creatively integrated, then the prognosis is good.

A greater need now exists to integrate sex and caring—to emphasize spirit in sex. More than ever, genitality should call for spirituality and spirituality for sexuality. We can also promote affective sexuality especially in appreciation of the other sex. We can be more relaxed and become more alike. A man can feel stronger and less afraid of being tender, gentle, and poetic. A woman can feel more liberated to take on so-called masculine activities. Especially after the crisis of middle age, we may experience fewer sexual differences in activities, interests, and mannerisms. The affective expression of sexuality becomes more similar rather than different in sexual relationships.

Actually, as we grow older, it is possible to become more sexual. Although genitality may decrease quantitatively, it can still be actively protected and promoted and/or creatively integrated. Moreover, we can grow more deeply in primary and affective sexuality.

Even the way we look and appear physically can in some ways be a call for spirit. Usually in late middle age we are no longer as physically attractive as we once were. Our skin begins to wrinkle, muscles lose tone, and physical shape usually worsens. Although these changes can be threatening without the spiritual, physical atrophy can be a challenge for the spirit. Even though we become less physically vigorous, we can show new spirit, depth, and vigor. Even though we cannot perform as well or as long, affective sexuality in terms of grace, gentleness, and tenderness can be a new form of vitality—sexuality permeated with spirituality. Thus, the hand that is becoming wrinkled can have more spirit than one that is twenty years old.

Still, it is possible to play sexual games at this time. A man, for example, may try to silence the haunting questions of the spirit that are often articulated in coming closer to death. He may frequent prostitutes or court younger women. Or a woman may pay younger men to escort her so she can run from the indictment of life—death. This voice of death speaks clearly and loudly as we grow older. Death is a demand to live more fully, to go beyond the periphery of living to the center of living, to integrate spirituality and sexuality. Thus, even though some older people still try to run from an authentic life, it gets increasingly difficult. Death calls forth the spirit of sex.

THE ELDERLY YEARS

As in the other passages of adulthood, three phases of the elderly years can be differentiated: an early, middle, and late phase. Physical, social, and personal factors contribute to being elderly. And to be elderly or old can mean to be as old as you feel. Some persons consider themselves in "late adulthood" until they become functionally dependent. To be sure, elderly adults vary considerably in their biological, psychological, social, and spiritual situations. And, as old people, they vary considerably in their sexuality.

To speak of sexuality in the elderly years may sound contradictory and even repulsive to us. To imagine wrinkled bodies making genital love makes many people uncomfortable. Nevertheless, we shall see that sexuality is an important experience in old age and genitality can also play a significant role. The main premises are that primary and affective sexuality, because they are contingent on being a whole person, should grow and mature more than ever. Although genital sexuality may decrease quantitatively, it too can deepen qualitatively—that is, be integrated in married or celibate life.

Shortly before and soon after retirement, we once again have a period of adjustment that can evoke stress. A homemaker, for instance, who does not have a career outside the home may go through a period of adjustment to becoming elderly and in adjusting to her spouse's retirement. And the celibate who retires from work (outside his or her community) usually has to make serious adjustments.

For many reasons, genitality usually decreases with old age. First of all, one's spouse is often not available. And though age is not a disease, disease that impedes genital relations is more prevalent in old age. Along with overall health, body concept is another significant factor in genital sexuality. Some old people become preoccupied with and fail to transcend their bodies; that is, they fail to accept and give deeper meaning to their bodies in terms of affective and primary sexuality. If we have centered ourselves on physical attractiveness, strength, or vigor, we probably will have difficulty in accepting bodily changes.

Excluding serious illness, a significant factor in genitality in old age is the previous history of genital experience and attitudes. If we have actively integrated genitality, we are more likely to make genitality meaningful. If genitality has been only a means to satisfy basic needs or has been repressed, genitality in the elderly years will probably be relatively rare and will not contribute to meaningful growth.

If we have not had genital relations in the past, genitality may not be much of an issue. For example, religious celibates who have led a celibate and chaste life may have experienced few ways to act genitally. However, if religious or lay celibates have repressed sexuality, sexuality may become an issue in the elderly years, sometimes in the form of explicit genital frustration which may be relieved and increased with masturbation. More often such repressed genitality manifests itself in the forms of insipid emptiness and lethargy. People who have repressed genitality throughout their life can end by becoming dried up.

In the middle phase of the elderly years, another personal crisis occurs, and it usually centers around an intimate confrontation with death. If we have confronted and learned from our past death and dying, we can embrace death more easily and fully than before. But for those of us who have escaped from death and have led mad lives, death can be devastating. If we run from death's indictment, paradoxically we may die before our time. An escape from death also means an escape from sexuality. Sex becomes lifeless.

Sometimes elderly persons may regress to an earlier state of development and consequently try to act as younger persons might. For instance, an elderly man may try to become intimate or play sexual games with a young woman, or an elderly woman might become amorous about a young man. Or such elderly people might periodically indulge in pornography and foster genital fantasies. This does not mean that elderly people cannot or should not be intimate with young people. Such involvement is healthy when integrated with and supportive of love.

Although we decline physically, we need not necessarily

decline psychologically and spiritually. And even if there is some psychological impairment such as brain damage, our spiritual life can still grow. Since spiritual life is embodied, we can grow in sexuality in the late sixties throughout the seventies, eighties, nineties, to death. Although physical capabilities are lessened and though there may be loss in intellectual functions, sexuality can nevertheless be deeper than ever.

At this critical time, death throws us back on ourselves. Can we as elderly persons come to a sense of reconciliation and integration—a serene wholeness? Specifically for our concern: Can we integrate and realize our sexuality? If we have lived a life of integrated (chaste) sexuality, then sexuality will almost invariably fall into healthy place.

At this time, we may become disenchanted with all kinds of sexuality, especially genital sexuality. In confronting life in terms of death, sexuality can be experienced as senseless. Genitality in particular may wain or come to a crisis because we often feel alone at this time and illness may occur. Nevertheless, there are few excuses to exclude genitality completely. Indeed, genital potency has declined but such a decline does not necessarily mean a decline in sexual desire or an inability to have genital intercourse.

Outside the genital realm, we can promote affective sexuality more than ever. We can become more sensitive to and appreciative of life. Compassion can be fully realized. We love in a compassionate way—suffer with and for others, a way that is intensely embodied and therefore sexual. We can be very affectionate without it leading to genital intercourse, and our intimacy may not even involve physical touching. A loving glance or smile can be a deep mode of affective sexuality. In the elderly years, the spirit lives and life can breathe more freely than ever.

In the late phase of elderly adulthood, we may not "feel very old" but nevertheless we are usually treated as very old. If we have grown through the current of life, we will reach the climax of our lives. But for those of us who have run from growth experiences and have violated life with sexist and exploitative procedures, our lives will slowly run out in despair. As "old elderly" people, we can come to the zenith of our sexuality. But there are often subtle pressures on us to minimize sexuality especially genitality, and such social attitudes can be internalized so that we impede ourselves. We can fulfill our own prophecies and think that sexuality is "not for old people."

Genitality can be actively significant in the elderly years, and more chaste in that it can be purely integrated in self and others. Genitality can call forth and promote the spiritual by spontaneous sublimation and respectful integration, and thereby give us vitality and enthusiasm. And we are unlikely to focus on or be seduced by physical genitality; instead, we can consciously, spontaneously, and respectfully integrate genitality so that we "see" and appreciate the beauty of ourselves and others. The spirituality of genitality can reach its culmination in the elderly years.

Existential and affective sexuality can and should continue its maturing process. Older men often become more receptive and nurturing than younger men. They become more gentle and open to sexual promptings, and they can continue to develop abstract and cognitive coping abilities, especially if they have little or no brain damage. In a similar way, older women can become more receptive and open to aggressive and individual drives while continuing to nurture their affective and expressive ways of coping with reality.

We can become vitally beautiful persons in our elderly years when sexuality is integrated. Even though our bodies may be disintegrating, we can show a new grace and sensitivity. Our elderly touch can decidedly be a human (sexual) touch. When we witness to the deeper values of sexuality, however, we may threaten younger people who identify sexuality with reproduction and pleasure. Elderly people can indict normally mad views and practices of sexuality.

It is interesting to note that the sexes are more alike and more in harmony in the first and last years of life. It seems that as old people we can come back to our origins. This is not to say that elderly people are the same as children or that we necessarily regress, but that we participate more wholly and fully in humankind and transcend sexual dichotomies, prejudices, and any factors that prevent sexual integrity. In some ways it can be socially easier for us in old age because people are not so likely to pressure us to follow stereotypical sex roles. On the other hand, as old people, we may threaten all those who are not old because we are so close to death. Paradoxically, our being so close to death can inhibit others' sexuality, for we point out that sexuality is more basic and goes far beyond mere physical pleasure and functional reproduction. It is the elderly who can proclaim the spirit and beauty of authentic sexuality.

Selected Bibliography

BARDWICK, JUDITH M., ed. *Readings on the Psychology of Women*. New York: Harper and Row, 1972.

BERTOCCI, PETER A. *Sex, Love and the Person*. New York: Sheed and Ward, 1967.

BISCHOF, LEDFORD J. *Adult Psychology*. 2nd ed., New York: Harper and Row, 1976.

BLOOM, LYNN Z., COBURN, KAREN and PEARLWAY, JOAN. *The New Assertive Woman*. New York: Dell Publishing Co., 1975.

BREEMAN VAN, PETER G. "Unmarriageable for God's Sake." *Review for Religious*, vol. 34, no. 6, Nov., 1975, pp. 839-45.

BUBER, MARTIN. *I and Thou*. New York: Charles Scribner's Sons, 1958.

BUYTENDIJK, F.J.J. *Woman: A Contemporary View*. Translated by Denis J. Burrett. New York: Newman Press, 1968.

CARRINGTON, PATRICIA. *Freedom in Meditation*. Garden City: Anchor Press/Doubleday, 1978.

DECKARD, BARBARA SINCLAIR. *The Women's Movement. Political, Socioeconomic and Psychological Issues*. New York: Harper and Row, 1975.

DUBAY, THOMAS. "Celibacy as Fullness," *Review for Religious*. vol. 34, no. 6, Jan., 1975, pp. 88-100.

ERIKSON, ERIK H. *Childhood and Society*. New York: W.W. Norton and Co., 1963.

ERIKSON, ERIK H. *Identity: Youth and Crisis*. New York: W.W. Norton and Co., 1968.

FARRELL, WARREN. *The Liberated Man*. New York: Bantam, 1975.

FASTEAU, MARC FEIGEN. *The Male Machine*. New York: Dell Publishing Co., 1975.

FRAZIER, NANCY and SADKER, MYRA. *Sexism in School and Society*. New York: Harper and Row, 1973.

FROMM, ERICH. *The Art of Loving*. New York: Harper and Row, 1956.

GAGNON, JOHN H. *Human Sexualities*. Glenview, Ill.: Scott, Foresman and Co., 1977.

GOERGEN, DONALD. *The Sexual Celibate*. New York: The Seabury Press, 1974.

GREELEY, ANDREW. *Sexual Intimacy*. Chicago: The Thomas More Press, 1973.

GREER, GERMAINE. *The Female Eunuch.* New York: Bantam, 1972.

GRUMMON, DONALD L. and BARCLAY, ANDREW M., eds. *Sexuality, A Search for Perspective.* Princeton, New Jersey: D. Van Nostrand Co., 1971.

HAKENEWERTH, QUENTIN. *For the Sake of the Kingdom.* Collegeville, Minn.: The Liturgical Press, 1971.

HAMMARSKJOLD, DAG. *Markings.* Translated by Leif Sjoberg and W.H. Auden. New York: Alfred A. Knopf, 1964.

HAMMER, SIGNE. Women: *Body and Culture.* New York: Harper and Row, 1975.

HEIDEGGER, MARTIN. *Being and Time.* Translated by John Macquarrie and Edward Robinson. New York: Harper and Row, 1962.

HELICKA, IRENE M. *Empirical Studies in the Psychology and Sociology of Aging.* New York: Thomas Y. Crowell Company, 1977.

HITE, SHERE. *The Hite Report.* New York: Dell Publishing Co., Inc., 1976.

JOHNSTON, WILLIAM. *Silent Music.* New York: Harper and Row, 1974.

JUNG, C.G. *Psyche and Symbol.* Translated by Gary Baynes and R.F.C. Hull. Garden City: Doubleday and Co., Inc., 1958.

KALISH, RICHARD A. *Late Adulthood: Perspectives on Human Development.* Monterey, Cal.: Brooks/Cole Publishing Company, 1975.

KEANE, S.S. and PHILIP S. "The Meaning and Functioning of Sexuality in the Lives of Celibates and Virgins," *Review for Religious.* vol. 34, no. 2, March, 1975. pp. 277-314.

KEANE, S.S. and PHILIP S. *Sexual Morality.* New York: Paulist Press, 1977.

KIMMEL, DOUGLAS C. *Adulthood and Aging.* New York: John Wiley and Sons, Inc. 1974.

KOSNIK et al. *Human Sexuality, New Directions in American Catholic Thought.* New York: Paulist Press, 1977.

KRAFT, WILLIAM F. *The Search for the Holy.* Philadelphia: Westminster Press, 1971.

KRAFT, WILLIAM F. *A Psychology of Nothingness.* Philadelphia: Westminster Press, 1974.

KRAFT, WILLIAM F. "Sisters and Priests," *Sisters Today.* May, 1977.

KRAFT, WILLIAM F. "Celibate Genitality," *Review for Religious*. vol. 36, no. 4, July, 1977.

KRAFT, WILLIAM F. *Normal Modes of Madness*. New York: Alba House, 1978.

LAING, R.D. *The Politics of Experience*. New York: Pantheon Books, 1957.

LAKOFF, ROBIN. *Language and Woman's Place*. New York: Harper and Row, 1975.

LEPP, IGNACE. *The Psychology of Loving*. Baltimore: Helicon Press, 1965.

LEVINSON, DANIEL J. *The Seasons of a Man*. New York: Alfred A. Knopf, 1978.

LUIJPEN, WILLIAM A. *Existential Phenomenology*. Pittsburgh: Duquesne University Press, 1966.

MASLOW, ABRAHAM H. *Toward a Psychology of Being*. Princeton, New Jersey: D. Van Nostrand Co., 1962.

MASTERS, W.H. and JOHNSON, V.E. *Human Sexual Inadequacy*. Boston: Little, Brown & Co., 1976.

MASTERS, W.H. and JOHNSON, V.E. *Human Sexual Response*. Boston: Little, Brown & Co., 1969.

MASTERS, W.H. and JOHNSON, V.E. *The Pleasure Bond: A New Look at Sexuality and Commitment*. Boston: Little, Brown & Co., 1975.

MAY, ROLLO. *Love and Will*. New York: W.W. Norton and Co., 1969.

McCARY, JAMES LESLIE. *McCary's Human Sexuality*. New York: D. Van Nostrand Co., 1978.

McNAMARA, WILLIAM. *Mystical Passion. Spirituality for a Bored Society*. New York: Paulist Press, 1977.

McNEILL, JOHN J. *The Church and The Homosexual*. Kansas City: Sheed, Andrews and McMeel, 1976.

NEUGARTEN, BERNICE L., ed. *Middle Age and Aging*. Chicago: The University of Chicago Press, 1968.

OAKLEY, ANN. *Sex, Gender and Society*. New York: Harper Colophon Books, 1972.

ORAISON, MARC. *The Human Mystery of Sexuality*. New York: Sheed and Ward, 1967.

PABLE OFM. CAP and MARTIN W. "Psychology and Asceticism of Celibacy," *Review for Religious*. vol. 34, no. 2, March, 1975, pp. 266–276.

PETRAS, JOHN W., ed. *Sex Male, Gender Masculine.* New York: Alfred Publishing Co., Inc., 1975.

PIETROPINTO, ANTHONY and SUNENAUER, JACQUELINE. *Beyond the Male Myth.* New York: Times Books, 1977.

PLATTEL, MARTIN G. *Social Philosophy.* Pittsburgh: Duquesne University Press, 1965.

PLECK, JOSEPH H. and SAWYER, JACK. *Men and Masculinity.* Englewood Cliffs, N.J.: Prentice-Hall, Inc., 1974.

PLE, ALBERT. *Chastity and the Affective Life.*, Translated by Macie Claude Thompson, New York: Herder and Herder, 1966.

REEVES, NANCY. *Womankind: Beyond the Stereotypes.* New York: Aldine Atherton, Inc., 1971.

ROCK, AUGUSTINE, ed. *Sex, Love and the Life of the Spirit.* Chicago: The Priory Press, 1966.

RUETHER, ROSEMARY RADFORD, ed. *Religion and Sexism,* New York: Simon and Schuster, 1974.

SADLER, WILLIAM A. *Existence and Love: A New Approach in Existential Phenomenology.* New York: Charles Scribner's Sons, 1969.

SADOCK, BENJAMIN J., KAPLAN, HAROLD I, and FRIEDMAN, ALFRED M., eds. *The Sexual Experience.* Baltimore: The Williams and Williams Company, 1976.

SARGENT, ALICE G. *Beyond Sex Roles.* New York: West Publishing Company, 1977.

SCHILLEBEECKX, E. *Celibacy.* New York: Sheed and Ward, 1968.

SCHUTZ, ALFRED. *Collected Papers.* The Hague: M. Nijoff, 1962.

SHEEHY, GAIL. *Passages.* New York: E.P. Dutton and Co., 1976.

SHOPE, DAVID F. *Interpersonal Sexuality.* Philadelphia: W.B. Saunders Co., 1975.

SINGER, JANE. *Androgyny. Toward a New Theory of Sexuality.* Garden City: Anchor Press/Doubleday, 1977.

SORENSON, ROBERT C. *Adolescent Sexuality in Contemporary America.* New York: World Publishing Co., 1973.

STRONG, BRYON *et al.,* eds. *Human Sexuality: Essentials.* New York: West Publishing Co., 1978.

SULLIVAN, HARRY STACK. *The Interpersonal Theory of Psychiatry.* New York: W.W. Norton and Co., Inc., 1953.

TAYLOR, G. RATTRAY. *Sex in History.* New York: Harper Torch Books, 1970.

TILLICH, PAUL. *Love, Power, and Justice.* New York: Oxford University Press, 1954.

TROLL, LILLIAN. *Early and Middle Adulthood.* Monterey, CA: Brooks/Cole Publishing Company, 1975.

VANDER, KERKEN L. *Loneliness and Love.* Trans. J. Donceel. New York: Sheed and Ward, 1967.

VAN KAAM, ADRIAN. "The Fantasy of Romantic Love," *Modern Myth and Popular Fancies.* Pittsburgh: Duquesne University Press, 1961.

VON HILDEBRAND, DIETRICH. *Man and Woman.* Chicago: Franciscan Herald Press, 1966.

WEBER, LEONARD M. *On Marriage, Sex, and Virginity.* New York: Herder and Herder, 1966.

WEIDEGGER, PAULA. *Menstruation and Menopause.* New York: Dell Publishing Co., 1977.

WEINBERG, GEORGE. *Society and the Healthy Homosexual.* Garden City: Anchor Press/Doubleday, 1973.

WILLIAMS, JUANITA H. *Psychology of Women. Behavior in a Biosocial Context.* New York: W.W. Norton and Company, 1977.

ZUBIN, JOSEPH and MONEY, JOHN, eds. *Contemporary Sexual Behavior: Critical Issues in the 1970's.* Baltimore: The John Hopkins University Press, 1973.